YOU DON'T HAVE TO BE DEAD IF YOU'RE EIGHTY

BARBARA NUGENT

WHIMSICAL MEANDERINGS of an OCTOGENARIAN

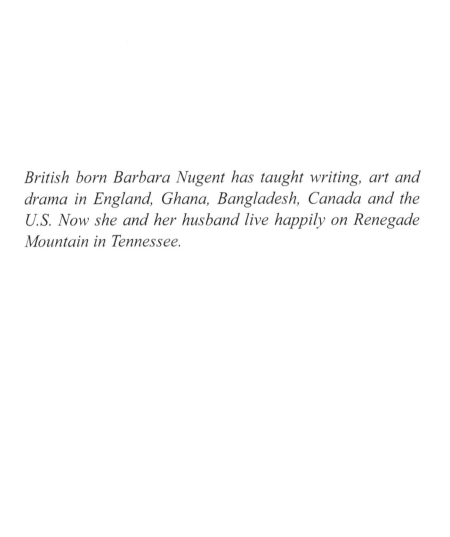

British born Barbara Nugent has taught writing, art and drama in England, Ghana, Bangladesh, Canada and the U.S. Now she and her husband live happily on Renegade Mountain in Tennessee.

ACKNOWLEDGEMENTS

To my humorously tolerant husband and children who, having no chance to vet my stories, have trusted me enough to allow me to write about their part in my life . . . (please don't sue me!)

To my generous sons, Greg and Giles, for their constant tolerance at my lack of computer capability . . .

To my remarkable grandson, Eamonn, who has helped me fix my multitude of errors . . .

To Yvette, my so-special daughter-in-law, for her patience and hours of meticulous editing . . .

To all those wonderful people who, across the panorama of the last eighty years, have woven such brilliant colors in the fabric of our travels . . .

To my faithful clientele here in Crossville and other loyal friends whom I've not been able to include in my stories, you have supported me so kindly . . .

And particularly, to my mother, long gone, who taught me how to laugh at myself and value the creation of happiness.

My heartfelt thanks.
You are all dearly loved.
I have been blessed.

Dedication

Over the years, my mother wrote articles and short stories but only one novel. This she did in secret when she was sixteen and proudly showed her manuscript to her mother.

"Waste of time," she was told, and it was promptly thrown into the fire. "You obviously don't have enough chores to do."

This to me was an appalling tragedy. How could a mother be so unfeeling and cruel? But it was just one example of the sad childhood my beloved mother endured. It resulted in her determination that nothing like that would ever happen again, so when she grew up, she published in secret.

To this day, I still don't know her nom de plume and have only one story and a few scattered notes to remember her by. Perhaps my meanderings will compensate just a little for what my family has lost.

AL MEANDERINGS of an OCTOGENARIAN

...eard that life is a bowl of cherries; perhaps a better
...jar of sweet-sour pickles. I know mine has been a
...experiences: some, less than happy, but as I look
...hat I remember is filled with laughter and sunshine.
...a product of our environment, so they say. Now that's
...nent, but having had a happy childhood growing up
...loving parents, I basically had little fear and knew
...as a curiosity waiting to be explored.
...lore it, I did. At the age of seven, not once, but
...n succession, I tested the ice on a frozen cow pond
...smothered in mud . . . and goodness knows what
...time I remember being smacked!
...didn't cure me. In the summer, the bluebell wood
over the ... the hill was our favorite haunt. Deliciously squelchy
streams just begged to be waded through. I think I must often have
been the despair of my mother who would have loved a dainty, de-
mure daughter. Instead, she had a tom boy, a harum-scarum child
who just knew the world was her playground.

Even when I was grown, married, with a family, I still loved
playing in the mud.

When the children were small, we lived near a steep hill
where a waterfall-like stream tumbling over broken rocks. The Hundred Steps, we called them. During the summer vacation, after a
heavy rain storm, I would take the children and some of their friends,
all in their oldest clothes, and scramble down those rocks getting
thoroughly soaked. Such fun. We would come home gloriously
filthy, but so content.

I remember writing back to my parents in England and telling them about our explorations.

"Typical," was my father's comment. He reminded me how I
never did seem to have much decorum, how he had despaired that I
would ever grow up to be a lady, for as a child I rushed about, rarely
looking where I was going, happy-go-luckily dancing through life.

He reminded me of another childhood experience, which
was so typical of me.

When I was about eight, I was chasing our pet guinea-pig
across the kitchen floor. I tripped over it . . . and dived right through
the glass door into the hall.

1

Blood everywhere. Luckily, the cuts looked much worse than they were. But on my wrist I still have a horseshoe scar where my father took the sliver of skin I had sliced off and stuck it back in place with plaster. Instant surgery.

I remember wondering why nobody seemed to be particularly cross about the broken glass. I expect my mother must have taken it all in her stride and found something to be happy about; the damage to me could have been worse. Just as well that smiles and laughter were the ingredients of her approach to life, ones I have tried to emulate. Sunshine beats gloom any time. But she, too, must have wondered if I would ever grow up.

And I don't suppose I ever have.

SEVEN

Another earlier memory, another learning experience, is still vivid. At the time it was so serious. It's rather trivial, but it has colored my life.

I was barely four and was sitting on the step at the front door of our house watching my mother who was in the garden pruning a tree. I was apparently thinking deep thoughts. I finally asked a question.

"I wonder what it will be like to be grown up? Really grown up, like seven?"

Of course, my mother laughed. I was furious. I put my little head down on my knees and felt blazing, silent anger. My mother had laughed at me!

Now I knew that seven was not really grown up, but it was as far as my little mind could conceive. My big brother Michael was seven and I adored him. I had been totally serious, and my mother had no right to laugh.

But though her humor was quite understandable, there and then I made a promise to myself, I would never laugh AT anyone, ever.

I didn't tell my mother how I had felt that day until many years later, at which stage she ruefully apologized; but I assured her what a lesson it had taught me. Quite often I would tell this story, particularly to my older students. So many of them had little self confidence and needed the assurance that their mistakes would never be laughed AT. Scorn can be such an ugly weapon used too often in the classroom, so I would avoid it, going in the opposite direction.

"Mistakes are the most important things you can do in the course of learning. Never be afraid to make them; you will not only remember them at the end of the day, but you will also remember the correct answers. We teachers have no right to laugh AT you, or AT those mistakes."

Of course, my rather prideful pontification did come back to haunt me. Daughters do keep one from becoming too smug.

As our children were growing up, we regularly drove past a particular tree that had a great gouge taken out of it to allow space for telephone wires. "Look, there's the greedy cookie monster . . ." We'd all laugh.

Many years later Rowena told me how she was scared to death of that tree and used to dream about it coming to eat her.

3

I had no idea how painful our laughter was to my sensitive child, or that the oft-repeated, stale joke was something she dreaded.

In a different way, I had been just as guilty as my mother all those years ago, and as insensitive.

I, too, most humbly apologized.

CONTRASTS

Though my mother's sunshine attitude has colored my life, living most of my childhood in Yorkshire, there were wet and windy days when it didn't stop raining, definitely gloomy, and we shivered.

I do remember having chilblains on my heels, mainly because our school classrooms were each heated by big fires at the front, while the back areas were icy North Poles. Only the good children could sit near that fire, so according to our behavior, we could be shunted backward and forward; hence, the chilblains.

But we all suffered the same, so it was no use complaining. Anyway, it was certainly an incentive to good behavior.

Another incentive to good behavior was when each morning the headmaster came into our classroom and drilled us on our tables. We stood to attention as he walked up and down the aisles, listening for mistakes. It was a point of honor to be the last one still on one's feet, which ensured a seat near the fire.

I remember there were some children who never made it to the front, poor souls. They anguished through the inquisition, knowing they would quickly be forced to sit down and spend another day at the back . . . in that icy cold.

The chanting of those tables still associates in my mind with extremes of comfort and discomfort; but I can hardly deplore the cruelty of the experience when I listen to modern youngsters who cannot even work out change at a cash register without a calculator. I can still repeat the sing-song cadence we used, and I slip into it if I need to jog my memory . . . six sevens are forty-two; seven sevens are forty-nine . . . Of course, today I would never sing out loud . . .

But I suppose I should thank that martinet of a headmaster for his tough but rewarding learning experience; even the chilblains were part of it, for they, too, had been an incentive to that learning.

THE TABLE

The second year of the war, that particular September was glorious. Lovely hot days, bright blue skies. As a small child, I thought the world was a wonderful place, not aware that the Battle of Britain was taking place, often over our heads.

I and my two brothers would gaze up into the sky fascinated by the tiny airplanes up there going pop, pop, pop, at each other. Michael, my elder brother, all of four years older, would knowledgeable point out, "That one's a Messerschmitt, a Heinkell or a Dornier, one of the baddies." or "No, that's a Spitfire, or a Hurricane: a goodie," would argue Christopher David. The names dripped easily off our tongues. Perhaps one of the planes would go into a spiral dive and we'd try to guess, was it one of ours? But to me it was little more than a game. Oh, we'd all listen to the BBC news and hear Churchill's warnings, yet somehow, it never seemed real. Surely the 'dog fights' and the bombings would never touch us.

In the first month of the war, my father, a school master, had deliberately changed schools so he could move our family to the countryside, to a tiny village where surely we all would be safe from that evil man, Hitler.

As the war began to escalate, and German bombers, night after night, droned over the Channel to bomb London and other major industrial cities, my father was doubly glad he had moved us. Our sleepy little backwater was the last place to interest the Luftwaffe, but my parents made attempts at protecting us, just in case.

We had a large, rather hefty dining table that my father had made. He felt it would be a good place to hide under if danger should threaten. Naive, I suppose you could describe my parents, but there was no such thing as television to show us the devastation in the cities. Indeed, it was important to maintain the British 'stiff upper lip,' so Churchill's rallying cry of our invincibility convinced most of us that our puny efforts were quite enough to resist our enemy.

Of course, my mother, who was a great reader of the classics, must have been as phlegmatic as seventeenth century Samuel Pepys who wrote in his diary as he watched the Great Fire of London, "And so to bed." We, like him, were untouchable.

But each night, during a brief period when German bombers were blasting Hull, our nearest sea port, my mother tucked my two brothers and me into a makeshift sleeping arrangement under that

6

table. We grumbled, of course, there wasn't much room, but we thought it was a great giggle.

Then there came a night when even my imperturbable parents' belief in their security measures was shaken.

A German bomber, straying from its flight path, unloaded a land mine in the field at the side of our house. It scared the living daylights out of our two pet donkeys that had been snoozing quietly in the corner. They jumped the fence and were found the next day shivering in a neighbor's apple orchard, quite determined not to return.

But the blast from the explosion did more than frighten them. It blew out the rear windows in our house and brought down much of the ceiling in the dining room where we were sleeping.

Of course, the table collapsed.

My parents rushed down stairs from the other side of the house in horror at what they might find.

The only clear memory I have of that night was peering out through the dust and the rubble, laughing at my parents, saying, "Silly Daddy, your table wasn't as strong as you thought!"

Apparently, my mother cleaned us up as well as she could, (no water, of course), and sent us off to school. That dreadful man, Hitler wasn't going to get us down.

I don't supposed we talked about it to our friends. It was just another not very important wartime incident, for we had come through unscathed . . . even though that was the end of the life of the table. But I did so enjoy teasing my tough, invincible father. "See, I told you we'd be better in bed!"

The innocence and ignorance of childhood can put life into proportion, don't you think?

THE BATH

So many war time memories. . . .

We grew up quickly. We had to because of the shortages, But each of us was in the same boat, so we accepted the changes in our lives with little concern; indeed, much of these changes we thought of as a game. I remember how proud I was of the little flashlight bulb my father put into my gas mask box, which we had to carry at all times. It was not a toy, Daddy insisted, but I did enjoy flicking it on and off in the classroom; then smiling innocently at the teacher.

Yet events often shocked us out of our complacent cocoons. When the bombing of London started, many of the East-End-of-London children who lived in the dock area were evacuated. A large contingent came to our town, and I can remember waiting with my mother at the station for the train to arrive. For the last few days, the local women had been collecting blankets and mattresses to make temporary bedding in our church hall until the children could be farmed out to the various homes.

It was late when the train pulled in, much after my usual bedtime, and I was feeling a quite delicious sense of importance since I was going to be allowed to help.

My first shock came as I saw this straggling line of white-faced, thin, undernourished children with one adult supervising each half-a-dozen or so. No mothers or fathers. Exhaustion, bewilderment . . . and silence. I hadn't expected this. The children I played with were noisy, well-fed, happy-go-lucky.

Attached to their coats, each child had a brown, cardboard luggage-label on which had been printed their name and address, and they carried a small case or paper bag which contained their few possessions.

We herded them together, taking little hands in ours, and shepherded them to the church where hot cocoa and sandwiches were waiting.

I was allotted one little boy who was probably about eight, and I was told to get him ready for bed. Putting on my best motherly smile (I was all of twelve), I sat him down to help him undress.

Now I hit my first snag.

"Whatcha doin'? Leave me clothes alone."

"But you have to change. Let me help you find your paja-mas." I reached for his dilapidated bag.

"'Jammers, ain't got no 'jammers."

8

"Then what do you wear at night?"

"Same as I got on."

All right, I thought. He came from a different world from mine, so I wasn't going to argue. At least he allowed me to take off his shoes. I tucked him in and tried to cheer him up with conversation about the farm to which he was going, about the wonderful animals, etc.

"I got a h'animal," he volunteered.

"Oh yes. What is it?" I expected a cat or dog.

"I got a donkey."

A bit nonplussed, I asked him to tell me more.

"He sleeps wiv me. He's my pal."

Ah. It must be a toy. Poor little chap, he probably was missing it. There had been no toy in that pathetic bag of clothes. I reached for a teddy bear someone had donated and gave it to him.

"G'aarn. That's for kids. I ain't a baby."

"Oh, sorry, but since you didn't bring your donkey . . ."

"Ain't you got no sense, he got to pull the 'barrer' for me dad."

Oh dear. I was getting into deep water. Did he mean a real donkey?

"But a live donkey can't sleep with you."

" 'E do an all. Right next to the baff."

"The . . . er baff?"

"Yeh. Tub where me dad keeps the coals."

I was well and truly flummoxed.

"Go to sleep, Tommy."

I tucked him in and went to find one of the women who had come with the children. I needed a translation.

"Oh yes, it's quite true. His father has a barrow that the donkey pulls, and the only bathroom these houses have is outside where the donkey sleeps. Some of those people do store the coal in the bathtub!" She told me that the heat of the animal kept that small room warm in winter, which was why little Tommy liked to sleep there.

It all seemed so reasonable as she explained it, but I often wondered how he adapted to indoor plumbing and a barn full of animals at the farm, which was to be his new home.

Many years later, I was in London doing research for a thesis on housing problems. I climbed to the high walkway at the top of St Paul's and looked down on the new developments in what had been the devastated dock area. The old streets where Tommy must have

9

begun life were long gone; what had not been bombed had been torn down and high-rise apartments built in their place. I wondered about that old donkey, and the 'barrer' he had pulled. Had those evacuated children returned?

I had permission from the local council to talk to the residents of these flats: all part of my thesis, and I asked what had happened to the families who had lived in that area.

"Ee, they give us these 'ere flats, and right nice they be, much better than them thar back-to-back 'ouses. But it's like our old streets. They give us the same neighbors."

Apparently, a humane authority had given priority to those who had lost their homes and, as far as possible, created the same streets on the various floors of the apartment blocks.

I asked about the evacuated children and was told most of them had come back to their old homes as soon as the war was over. It had been an unsettled time, for whole streets had been destroyed and families separated. But with the extraordinary resilience of the Cockney, neighbor helped neighbor, and the old street clans survived.

I wished I could have found out about Tommy, whether he, too, had returned. And whether he had bought another donkey and become a 'barrer' boy like his dad. I had a feeling that that feisty little boy would have been a survivor and would not have forgotten how he had loved that first donkey.

But I don't suppose he would have been able to keep a new one next to the bath!

WAR TIME SHORTAGES

Children take life for granted. We knew we were rationed, but it didn't seem to affect us very much. It wasn't until years later that I truly understood how my mother starved herself in order to feed us. She rarely sat down to a hot meal with us, saying she wanted to get the clearing up done. It seemed a normal thing to do. She would eat later, usually potatoes and other vegetables. I just thought she preferred them to roast beef.

I remember recently teasing my college students who were complaining about the cost of double cheese burgers.

"Let me tell you just what we had during the war." I reeled off my list, "Each week we were allowed, four ounces of meat, four ounces of butter, four ounces of margarine, four ounces of sugar, and one egg." I enjoyed rubbing it in. That was enough to make them groan, particularly the one who had just eaten his double cheese burger with its half a pound of beef.

Other foods were rationed; bread, milk and canned foods. But we made up with vegetables from my mother's garden. I even grew to like brussels sprouts and cabbage.

In other areas, the shortages were hard to a growing teenager. Each of us had ration coupons for clothes. They just about covered one complete outfit a year. Casual shirts and shorts were impossible to have. I had my school uniform, which I wore for five years. It was a lovely blue and was made of beautiful, fine serge. I would take it off as soon as I came into the house so it could be sponged clean if necessary, and each autumn, my mother would let down the hem. That uniform had to last.

But we found all sorts of ingenious ways to augment our clothes. My father from somewhere got hold of a silk parachute. I had silk blouses, silk underskirts, even a silk nightie. And what was left over, my mother made into kitchen curtains.

This was when I learned to sew. 'Make do' was a phrase used as often as 'no more coupons'.

Then, toward the end of the war, I received a glorious windfall. My Great Aunt Emma died and left me her wardrobe.

When this plethora of garments arrived I wondered what on earth I could do with them. Great Aunt Emma was a tiny slip of a woman, and I was growing taller by the minute. As I unpacked the various items, I realized they were almost Victorian in length. Skirts to the ankles, with froths of equally long white petticoats to go un-

11

derneath. These had rows and rows of lace with pretty ribbons threaded through.

Really. What use were they to me?

Then I had an inspiration. My waist was about the size of Great Aunt Emma's hips.

I got out the scissors and snipped at that level!
A wonderful rich-brown coat with buttons all the way down the front became a skirt. It had tiny pinch pleats allowing for a delicious flair.

I was in business.

I did the same with the petticoats. With just the tiniest edge of lace peeping under the hem, and the fullness making my skirt swirl out, I was sure I looked like any Hollywood film star. None of my friends had anything so lovely. Oh, I blessed dear Great Aunt Emma.

And there was more. I decorated my plain, practical winter coat with an obviously rare and expensive mink collar. I made unusual ascot-like ties out of yards of broad, woven silk ribbons, and cut up a long, embroidered evening gown to make a church-going dress for my mother. She had had nothing new for years and deserved a little brightness in her life.

So we contrived and made do, but my over-riding memory was of the delight we found in making something out of nothing.

I had one particular success of which I was inordinately proud.

Daddy had a really good suit that no longer fitted him; my mother was going to find some worthy soul to whom to give it. After begging and pleading, with some skepticism from my parents, I was allowed to see what I could do with it.

Did you know that a man's suit has twenty-seven pieces to it? I carefully unstitched it, washed and ironed each piece, then recutting . . . with my heart in my mouth I may say . . . contrived a new suit for myself.

It was a tremendous success. I wore that suit well into my college days, always feeling so smart . . . and not a little smug. And what gave me the most pleasure? It had cost me nothing.

THE AMERICAN SOLDIERS

What does a child know? We listen to others and often judge by the superficial.

In 1942, the Yanks came to town. How resplendent they looked in their beautifully-fitting, gaberdine uniforms and with their endless supplies of chewing gum and cigarettes. Our British Tommies had very little, and their uniforms were scratchy, ill-fitting and unromantic.

Is it any wonder that the girls looked at these strangers with stars in their eyes? The Yanks had money and would happily pay for a good time.

And thus began a love-hate relationship.

Staunchly protective of their own, most of the older women were less welcoming than they should have been and did not encourage fraternizing with the foreigners. It was rather sad to hear them giving the cold shoulder to these men who had come over to help protect us.

I remember one of the rare occasions when my mother lost her temper. She had given afternoon tea to a group, as she did indiscriminately to any of the soldiers who needed a little home comfort. A rather grumpy, narrow-minded women told her just what she thought of her actions.

"Ee; thee's panderin' to them thar Americis. Send 'em back, I says."

"And where would we be if we did?"

My mother let her have it with both barrels. We had just endured the Battle of Britain and knew how desperately we needed American aid. Their joint effort with the R.A.F. in bombing Germany and ridding our skies of the Luftwaffe had saved so many British lives.

But ostrich-like, head-in-the-sand, this unkind animosity never quite died out until the invasion of France. Even then, it was only grudgingly agreed we couldn't have done without the Americans. I know patriotism has its place, and staunch support of one's own is commendable, but all men are equal in battle.

There was one time, though, when the British noses were rubbed in the mud.

When a contingency of Americans had first arrived at an airbase near my grandmother's village, many of them wanted some sort of transport other than their jeeps. Even they couldn't get unlimited petrol.

So they bought bicycles.

I'm ashamed to say some of the locals forced a hard bargain and sold their own bikes for much more than they were worth.

At the end of the war, the Americans tried to sell them back, allowing for wear and tear, at what seemed to them to be a reasonable price. Of course, their offers were refused. The Yanks couldn't take the bikes with them to the States, so the wily British thought they could pick them up for nothing.

Not pleased, the Americans had a better idea.

They laid them out in a long line at the side of the aerodrome runway and bulldozed over the lot, leaving a pile of useless scrap metal.

Half the village was a mad as hell; the other half secretly chuckled at the tit-for-tat action.

But this silly animosity was based on more than uniforms and bikes.

All during the war, we children had no ice cream. I don't suppose it did us any harm, and I don't remember feeling particularly deprived. But the Americans on their airbases had as much as they wanted . . . flown in courtesy of Uncle Sam.

I suppose it was understandable that mothers should feel a certain amount of resentment. Perhaps Uncle Sam had been less than wise in providing that ice cream, though surely they deserved it. And to be fair, many parties were given by those Americans for local children where those goodies were shared. Those service men really were so kind.

But the saddest thing of all was the bewilderment of these same Americans who had courageously left their own families to fight a war that was not of their making yet were given the cold shoulder by those narrow-minded few.

That damned ice cream and those pretty uniforms!

I suppose it is just human nature to resent those who have more: a reverse dog-in-the-manger attitude, but it certainly sullied what should have been a relationship of gratitude. Of course, attitudes matured, for we know we probably would have lost the war without the unselfish devotion of those men who came to protect and save a devastated Europe.

I'm thankful my parents did not allow that ignorance to color our family's association with the Americans . . . though I remember I never told my father that I went to one of the dances given by them. I had a wonderful time.

Delicious fun.

A thousand Americans and a dozen girls!

My father's generosity of spirit only went so far! And he, too, had always liked ice cream.

THE BLANKET

One bitter December toward the end of the war, my mother was at her wit's end to keep her family warm; indeed, though most of England was shivering, in the North, high on the Yorkshire moors, it always seemed so much colder than the rest of the country. With no central heating and limited rations of coal, keeping cozy in our morgue of a house was tough.

The nights were the worst. Simple things that now we take for granted, such as extra blankets for our beds, were impossible to replace. Ration coupons were so limited that they could not be spent on new bedding, even if such were available in the stores. Extreme measures were needed to keep body and soul together.

Now my ever-ingenious mother never sat down and moaned; she always tried to find a solution, whatever the problem.

It was nearly Christmas, and we all needed some sort of spark to bring alive the holiday spirit. What better than a family activity?

She spread on the living room floor an old, worn-out sheet and sat my brother and me around it. (My older brother by now was serving in the army.) Next, she took from a closet no-longer-useable pieces of material: ragged oddments of blanket and old drapes. My mother threw nothing away, for we never knew what might come in useful, or how long the war would last. Carefully overlapping these scraps on the sheet, she covered them with another, equally worn, but whole piece of blanket.

Now it was our turn. Giving us each bodkin needles threaded with brightly colored wool, she instructed us to stitch in wild, random patterns all through the pile, making sure no piece was left loose. We created funny faces, odd shaped animals, and surrealistic flowers, with plenty of crooked lines in between. When we had finished, my mother stitched all round the edge to make sure our strange blanket didn't fall apart. It was a hilarious evening, our youthful minds delighting in our artistic efforts.

Of course, we had to give our concoction a name, and thus began the life of our Joseph blanket. We had been brought up on Bible stories and knew all about Joseph's coat of many colors. During that winter, and later ones until the end of rationing, we children used to fight over whose turn it was to have that blanket on our bed, for it was so thickly layered that it was the warmest in the house.

16

I had forgotten about that much loved, cozy covering until many years later when I was clearing my mother's house after she died. I was searching through cupboards to see what could be given to Good Will. I opened a drawer and found in it two brand-new blankets, still in their cellophane wrappers. These we had bought as Christmas presents some years before, but my mother, who always saved for a rainy day, had never opened them. I remember smiling sadly at her frugality. I moved them to one side.

In a corner, neatly folded, beside these untouched bundles, was our old Joseph blanket.

I sat down and cried.

There was something almost poetic about the old and the new, kept so carefully, obviously both cherished. The bright wool had faded, but the amusing stitches brought back so vividly that winter evening and the fun we had, and the joy my mother always managed to bring to our family, even when conditions were at their worst.

To me, that old blanket was far more valuable that those pristine, store-bought ones.

And I believe my mother kept it, too, because equally, to her, its value was beyond price.

THE GIFTS

England, early spring, 1945.

We had known almost six years of war. Hardship had beaten down morale, tempers were frayed, and any uplifting of spirit was difficult. By the end of that winter, we were all so fed up with shortages, rationing, and the dull, dreary, black-out nights.

Surely peace must come soon.

But the weeks dragged on. It became tougher to raise a smile or crack a joke. Even we children were subdued and rarely laughed.

"Enough!" said my mother. She was in charge of our Sunday school and realized that something must be done. The Church Anniversary was coming up, and in order to brighten our lives she decided that we should have a pageant. A colorful, sparkling pageant, with lots of dressing up. Children always love that.

Of course, we had to have an appropriate theme; and since we all were being encouraged to look forward to the end of war with hope, and definitely forgiveness of our enemy, that became our high-sounding motto.

"Let the People of the World Unite in Faith, Hope and Charity."

Each child was to recite some touching verse on those uplifting words. All were to be clad in costumes to represent as many nations as possible and carry a gift to the altar. My mother was determined to create a few moments of joy.

Strong lady, my mother.

Understandably, the children's parents could hardly be expected to come up with anything so frivolous as costumes, for nothing was available in the stores, and few had clothing coupons to spare. So my mother ransacked our own home to provide garments that would represent people of other lands. Wearing these, our Sunday school children were to dramatize the theme of the pageant, Faith, Hope and Charity throughout all lands.

I can't say I was feeling too charitable, for my pretty, blue silk bedspread had gone to make an Indian sari. I didn't have much hope of it being returned in its usual pristine condition, but all in a good cause, grudgingly I had agreed.

Two of the more rambunctious boys were to be nomadic Bedouins of the desert. For their outfits, even my mother was stumped. Then she had a brain-wave.

Black-out curtains.

18

They hung at each window throughout the house, and we were all heartily sick of the sight of them. Surely the pair from the guest bedroom would not be needed since the longer evenings of summer would soon be with us. These drapes were of heavy, dark material to be discarded as soon as the war was over when no longer would we have to black out indoor lights; surely that had to be soon. And no one was going to use that bedroom, anyway.

So we thought.

Unexpectedly, the afternoon before the Sunday Anniversary Pageant, my autocratic, humorless Grandmama arrived. My frazzled mother, still trying to put together the last pieces of various costumes, was not exactly pleased; but in the spirit of the morrow—Faith, Hope and Charity, etc., she did her best to make the old lady comfortable.

The guest room was prepared; a hot water bottle placed between the cold sheets, for bitter winds from the Arctic blew across our Yorkshire moors, and the limited fuel we were allowed did not stretch to heat in the bedrooms. Our meagre food rations were augmented to feed one extra; and to please Grandmama, a more elegant meal than my mother had intended was provided.

Eventually, so to bed.

Apologetically, my parents explained about the lack of drapes (now Bedouin cloaks) and asked Grandmama not to put on the bedroom lights. Black-out regulations were still rigidly in force. In the dark, the irritated old lady fumbled through her nightly preparations, and we all settled down to sleep.

Suddenly, a banging of doors and screams rent our peace.

"Rats, rats! There are rats in my bed."

You can imagine the speed with which we all left our rooms; my parents, in horror, I, in some glee. Grandmama was not my favorite person.

My parents flew across the landing, past the old lady who was trembling with indignation. The light, in spite of rules and regulations, was switched on, and the bed covers were thrown back.

There in the middle was a pile of small, sleek, moving bodies!

Earlier that evening, having found the bedroom door open and a cosy haven, Penelope, our cat, had burrowed under the bed covers and presented our guest with her latest batch of kittens.

Understandably, to Grandmama, these gifts of Faith, Hope and Charity (as they were eventually called) were too much.

19

Profuse with apologies, desperately trying to hide her amusement, my mother hastily removed proud Penelope and her off-spring to a box in the kitchen where it was warm. But of course, nothing could be done that night about the bed. I was relegated to a down-stairs sofa while a mumbling, grumbling, discombobulated old lady took my room. I suppose I deserved the discomfort since I had laughed out loud, but it was worth it.

The next morning, in high dudgeon, Grandmama departed. Even my father, whose mother she was, seemed not too displeased.

The rush of that Sunday continued. The pageant was a success, and I like to think that all my mother's efforts to bring a little color to our drab lives did, indeed, strengthen our belief in the gifts of Faith, Hope and Charity.

Later that evening, we collapsed in satisfied exhaustion and mulled over the events of the weekend. It was only then we realized that Penelope, our very proud cat, had given back to us an essential gift we had almost forgotten: one that had lain too long under the strain of war. But it was one we never again allowed to be far from us during those last months before the armistice . . . the joyous, uninhibited gift of laughter.

SCHOOL AND MAD MAX

I'm sure everyone's teen years are colored by memories of teachers. During the war, so many were called up and replacements were often untrained. But my first year in grammar school (the equivalent of seventh grade in an American high school) I had a math teacher I shall never forget. Mad Max, we called him. Max Miller was beyond the age of conscription, for which we students were extremely grateful.

Mad Max was a character. He believed passionately in his subject and used every gimmick to bring to life what to most children was dull and boring. Long dark hair; vivid, sparkling eyes; he would stride down the corridor, his black gown swirling behind him, just like a magnificent crow. But we never laughed at him. Even in our childish minds, we knew he was special.

I'll never forget the day he taught us about tangents and arcs.

He came into the classroom and immediately climbed onto a desk and proceeded to walk across the line of them beside the windows. He reached to the quarter-moon, upper panes slamming them open, then shut. The ratchet bars that held them in place slid backward and forward. He began to chant, "Arc . . . tangent. Tangent . . . arc."

I also remember, he refused to let us learn by heart Pythagorus' theorem. "Understand it! Understand it!" he would bark at us, creating an action play where we each took the part of a line or square or angle.

That year, I loved math and determined to be a math teacher when I grew up. Sadly, my father was transferred and I went to another school where the teacher seemed to know less than I did. Typical of any child in these circumstances, I became bored, disinterested, and to this day, my husband adds up my check book!

This transfer put me into a class where German had been taught the previous year. I had done the obligatory first-year Latin and French, but no German. Nobody bothered to find out, and I was too much in awe of the teacher to admit my complete ignorance. She was over six feet tall, with a tongue like a whip.

I only remember two remarks of hers. One was, "Barbara, you have the perspicuity of a cow!" (I had no idea what she meant), and the other was a comment she put on my report card. "Barbara is trying!" I knew perfectly well she didn't mean I was making an effort.

21

The third teacher I remember: I caused him no little embar-rassment. I was in the upper sixth (the senior year) and no longer had to wear the school uniform; I wore a navy skirt and blouse instead. I was taller than most of the other girls and had learned to wear my hair in a roll round my head instead of a plait. I looked quite grown up, I thought.

Mr. Brown was a new teacher.

He stopped me as I was walking along the corridor and started to chat about this and that. Not minding that I might be late for class; after all, I had the perfect excuse, I chatted, too.

Eventually, he decided he'd better get to his new class and hoped he would see me later. Rather flattered, I probably agreed.

I collected my books from my locker and walked into the classroom to take my place. The teacher turned from the black board on which he had been writing and looked at me ready to chastise this student who was late.

Even now, over sixty years later, I can still remember the bright red blush on poor Mr. Brown's face . . . and the rather gleeful giggle I suppressed at having been thought to be a teacher!

LATER EDUCATION

Getting into college was tough. I had a scholarship, but 95% of all places were going to ex-servicemen. Most of the rest went to male students, and a measly fraction, to girls. Consequently, I taught at the local primary school for a year while I waited.

I was given a class of six-year-olds.

I remember one sweet little boy, Keith Young. He had large, limpid, blue eyes and the cutest cowlick, which he was always trying to flatten. He came from a very poor household; no father; a mother who cleaned houses to make ends meet.

I had a particularly soft spot for dear Keith; he always wanted to please and worked hard so his mother would be proud of him. I wondered what would become of him since in those days it was not easy to climb above one's station.

He was special, and I was touched that he was fond of his new teacher and often asked for a cuddle.

Thirty years later, my mother was in hospital having an operation. The extremely important head surgeon bustled in, and the nurses hastily tidied sheets and removed trays and medical paraphernalia. They apparently considered him to be the next best thing to God.

I stepped back. Relatives were less than important, obviously.

I got a brief nod.

Then a pause . . . a double take.

Gone was the authoritative manner.

"Miss Savage?" A hesitancy. An almost shy expression. "I don't suppose you remember me?" A rueful smile. "My favorite teacher."

I'm sure my smile stretched from ear to ear. The same cow lick, and the same limpid, blue eyes.

"Keith, Keith Young. Of course I remember you. My favorite student!"

It was quite a special moment; particularly to know the wonderful success he had made of his life. Did I play an important part? Probably not, but I like to think I had, at least, helped him a little.

ST. ALBANS CATHEDRAL

The college years rushed by: I'm amazed how little I remember. But it was a whole new world. Architectural studies, lectures, boy friends, silly parties, tennis and hockey matches, intensive design work, discovery of new places and people, and particularly the joy of exploring ancient buildings. Then further studies to enable me to teach. Fascinating work on two enormous theses. Life was indeed the proverbial bowl of cherries.

I chose to study St. Albans Cathedral for one of my theses and spent many happy hours exploring that extraordinary building. One of its claims to fame is that it took nearly 800 years to complete; thus, it is a hodgepodge of various architectural styles.

I became very friendly with the verger who allowed me to poke around in all sorts of hidden corners. In the center is a huge Norman tower. Behind it, where adjacent walls abutted it, was a dark corner where some of the mortar had crumbled. Very carefully, I dug out a little and had it tested.

I was fascinated at what I discovered. That little lump gave me a vivid picture of those early builders working in conjunction with the monks, for the binding material of that mortar was hair; donkey and horse hair, from their tails, no doubt, and human hair. I had no way of knowing whether straw was used in later mortar, but the picture my mind conjured was of dedicated barber shaving each monk's tonsured head, and the farrier saving every scrap of his animals' hair . . . It was a very tall tower.

I studied other cathedrals and found many poignant stories of those early builders who travelled from one holy place to another as each bishop could afford further extensions. In one such building, way up in a hidden corner, where a giant pillar supports the roof, is a delicately carved head of a small boy. This child apparently used to climb the rickety ladder to take his father his dinner where he worked on carvings the bishop had ordered. One day, his son fell. I don't suppose anyone cared very much, but imagine the father's secret sorrow as he carved the face of his dead child.

But those college years bring back so many much less serious memories.

During vacations I was a fruit picker, a victualing officer on a yacht, a governess, a chambermaid, a radio announcer; indeed, whatever I tried, I had a ball. I danced free in a wonderful world that was an exciting place.

. . . Though there is one memory I'd prefer to forget.

Recently, an old friend reminded of the hilarious gaff I made at a college lecture.

I was supposed to ask a question of the famous politician, Lord <u>Boyd Orr</u> who had been explaining to us the evils of communism.

Impressive, extremely erudite, but I have to admit, rather dull, perhaps even a little sleep inducing.

I had mulled over my sentence very carefully before I rose to my feet.

I began. "I wish to ask Lord Bore . . ."

Great explosions of laughter. I don't know who had the redder face, the college principal, his Lordship, or me. I'm sure I wished I could sink through the floor.

But laughter is a wonderful, memory-inducing thing, don't you think?

Reality did eventually rear its ugly head. I had to earn a living.

Funnily enough, I had never intended to end up teaching; my father was a teacher, my mother and grandmother both had been teachers; that was the last thing I intended to do. I think perhaps my fondness for little Keith had penetrated deeper into my heart than I had realized. To this day, I love being in the classroom and have never regretted it.

I started teaching in London but kept up my sports activities; I joined the local tennis club. I adored the game and played most weekends when the weather allowed

And then . . .

I suppose I should say this was when the rest of my life began . . .

THE MEETING

One miserable, wet, blustery March evening, instead of staying in my flat and doing the ironing as I intended, I decided to go down to the club to see my friends. There'd be music and dancing to cheer us up. It had been a long, cold winter and we all were longing for sunny days.

Peter, a casual boyfriend, had said he'd be coming in later, so I stood at the coffee bar talking to friends as I waited for him.

The door opened and a stranger walked in. He was muffled up against the cold in a heavy coat, but his head was uncovered and raindrops glistened on his dark hair. I looked at his unsmiling, autocratic profile.

Quite why, to this day, I don't know . . . I turned to the person standing next to me and said, "That's the man I should marry."

I remember feeling startled surprise, wondering what had hit me. Stupid comment. I had no idea who he was; certainly I had never met him before. Prosaic common sense reared its practical head and I turned away.

A few minutes later, someone called me from the other end of the bar.

"Oh, Barbara. I want you to meet Dickie; he's waiting for Peter, too."

I looked up to see the stranger coming toward me, a frown on his remarkably handsome, bronzed face.

I who was always a chatterbox was struck dumb.

"Good evening," the man said.

I suppose I said 'good evening' back. I don't remember. I think we talked about the weather, or maybe he did. But I do remember standing there like a dummy. Finally, probably in desperation, Dickie asked of I would care to dance. We rather woodenly moved around the floor until we saw Peter arrive.

Much relief on my part. Probably on Dickie's, too.

Greeting each other like long lost brothers, they laughed as they caught up on each other's news of old friends, "How's old so-and-so?" " Did you hear about . . .?" I stood there, obviously easily forgotten and not of the least importance.

I gleaned bits of information. Dickie was home on leave from Africa; he and Peter had met over there. As they chatted on, dates to play tennis were made for when the weather improved.

At last, they remembered that I was standing there.

26

"Sorry," said Peter. "I'm afraid I have to get back to London," he had a restaurant there. "Dickie, will you take Barbara home?"

Damn. I hated being organized. And being palmed off onto another was not exactly complementary.

Dickie agreed. What else could he do?

He drove me back to my flat and said good night. That was it: nothing more: no polite thanks for a pleasant evening. Ah well. He was just a stranger, and what did I care?

That was Saturday. The following Tuesday my phone rang.

"Barbara? What are you doing this evening?" Truth to tell, I wasn't sure who was calling. I had forgotten this tall, dark and handsome stranger since he had shown no interest in this silent woman who had been thrust upon him.

"Er . . . my brother is here for dinner."

"How tall is he?"

" Six feet two, I think."

"Well, I'm six feet five; I'll pick you up in half-an-hour."

I'm sure my mouth hung open.

"What was that all about?" Michael asked.

I told him. Seeing my utter bewilderment, he laughed. "Are you sure you want to go out with him?" I suppose my face told its own story.

Dickie dropped Michael at a tube station and took me to the theater. During the interval, we went to the bar for a drink. I was still pretty silent; perhaps we could talk about the show.

No. Conversation from me was not even necessary. I found myself watching as a crowd of people milled round, all wanting to speak to Dickie at the same time. I tried to piece together just who was this man.

It seems he was quite a famous tennis player, obviously well known in this London crowd. I found myself shrinking away, wondering just why he had chosen me for his companion that evening.

Eventually, when the evening was over, Dickie took me home: still not much conversation. As he was about to leave he said. "We'll go out to dinner on Friday. I'll pick you up at nine. Glad rags." With a wave of his hand, he left.

Stunned, I tried to rationalize this autocratic man. Just who was he? A tennis player—an important one, apparently, on leave from Africa, that was it. I didn't even know his last name.

But Friday sounded good.

I had dates on Wednesday and Thursday. I cancelled them both. I got out my one and only evening dress and ironed it; I cleaned my apartment thoroughly. I made an appointment to have my hair done after school on Friday, and by that evening I was halfway between hope and despair.

"Do you have a radio?" were his first words he said when he arrived, looking gorgeously handsome in what I later discovered was a brand new suit. I showed him where it was and he switched it on. 'Hancock's Half-hour' was one of his favorite programs. I sat there like a lemon.

At last, big beaming smile as he switched off. "Are you ready?" If he had been someone I knew better, I'm sure I would have made a sarcastic comment.

We drove to Hatchetts on Piccadilly. Big welcome from the maitre d' who obviously knew him. We ordered dinner and wine and danced. At last I was beginning to find my tongue. Halfway through the evening, I was talking about Portofino where I was intending to spend my summer vacation.

He didn't seem to be paying much attention.

By now I was getting a little riled.

"Aren't you interested?" I asked.

"Yes, but you won't be going to Portofino this summer."

"Why not?" I blurted out.

"You'll be in Africa."

"What on earth will I be doing in Africa?"

"You'll be my wife. Come, let's dance."

Now I didn't know whether to say "Pardon?" or "Yes, please." or just ignore what I must have misunderstood.

So we danced.

I suppose we picked up some sort of conversation, but I don't remember. Eventually, I mentioned my father who had been ill.

"Why don't you go to see him?"

I must have said, ". . . too far; school on Monday; trains not easy."

"I'll take you." Cool, calm arrogance. "Send them a telegram." (My parents didn't have a phone.) "I'll pick you up tomorrow morning at nine." He handed me a bunch of loose change and I went over to the call box.

"Arriving Saturday afternoon with Dickie. Love, Barbara." Brief and to the point. But what else could I say? They couldn't be any more bewildered than I was.

28

Promptly at nine, he arrived and we drove the 200 miles north.

My father answered the door: all six feet seven of him. Even my arrogant driver blanched. Oh dear . . .

Of course, I needn't have worried. My parents were much too polite to ask questions. Thank goodness, for I have no idea how I would have explained him. I couldn't have said; 'No, I don't know who he is . . . I don't know what his last name is . . . I think he said something about marrying me. Yes, I only met him a week ago . . .' My stern, Baptist-lay-preacher-father (who had been engaged to my mother for five years before marrying her) was not known for sudden actions: deliberation was far more his style.

But we had a delightful week end, anyway. Dickie was all charm.

Just before we were to leave to return to London, he asked to speak to my father alone.

Ten minutes later there was a huge rumpus and Dickie, white faced, came into the hall where I was waiting. My furious father stormed behind him.

"Out of this house!" finger pointed to the door. Almost stuttering with rage, he shouted, "Over my dead body! You'll not marry my daughter!"

My mother and I just stood there in numb horror. We had no idea what had happened.

There was more.

"I will have no Catholic in this family!"

So that was it. If only I had known, I could have warned Dickie. My father had an absolute detestation of Catholics. Our house was across the road from a Catholic family to whom my father had never spoken in all the years we had lived there. It had never worried me; it was just something we took for granted, for dear Daddy was a devout Baptist soul who preached blood and thunder, an equally devout Anti-Papist. He would have made a marvelously fanatical 17th. century Puritan.

We had never discussed this deep-seated hatred—some childhood trauma I believe.

Oh dear. It got worse. He turned to me.

"If you leave with him, you need never darken these doors again."

Talk about a Victorian drama. I suppose it was almost funny. But I had to go. Dickie was my ride back to London. In any case, I had none of my father's bias. A Catholic could be as good as a Baptist, surely?

And so we left, Dickie with a face as black as thunder. And I . . . well, I hadn't been consulted. No question had been popped to me . . . and I still didn't know just who, actually, was this angry man.

Half way down the road, he drew the car to the side and tersely said, "I shan't ask you to marry me yet. You must come to terms with your father's demands."

That was that. When he dropped me at my flat and drove off, I wondered if it would be the last I would see of him.

Damn!

We both have chuckled many times at the comic-opera of those few weeks. Of course, he called me and took me out. I managed to overhear someone use his last name: Newgate, I thought. As for his first name, it must be Richard since Dickie is the diminutive for that.

So it seemed I might be marrying Richard Newgate.

It never occurred to ask him. I could hardly say, "Yes, I'll marry you. By the way, what's your name?"

We became engaged on April the first, just three weeks after we met. Only then did I discover that his name was actually Gerald Nugent!

And only then did his mother tell me that he had woken her up that first evening when he had seen me at the tennis club. He told her that he had met the girl he was going to marry.

It seemed that the strange lightning bolt that had hit me as I stood at the coffee counter had turned around and given him the same jolt.

We were married three months later. Sadly, my father did not come to the wedding. His religion would not allow him to bend that far. But he did send me a Bible in which he had written,

"May the best of the past be the worst of the future."

MAL DE MER

I suppose my husband would have to admit that he didn't particularly enjoy our honeymoon!

Our first day after our wedding, we were driving near Pool Harbor where the yacht on which I used to sail was floating a hundred yards off shore.

"Oh, may we go on board?" I asked eagerly. I knew lots of old friends would be there.

Now what can a new husband say to his bride?

I hailed and a dingy was sent to pick us up. A very small dingy, one that rocked in the minor turbulence of the waves. We reached the yacht and climbed aboard. I went below, but Gerald didn't follow. I presumed he was enjoying the sea air.

Oh dear. When I came back on deck, he was not enjoying it at all: he was hanging over the rail as sick as a dog. And going back to shore in that little dingy didn't help. I felt so guilty; if only I had known that he was a poor sailor . . .

But the sheer indignity of my husband's *mal de mer* didn't end there.

A few days later, we began the second part of our honeymoon, the twelve-day trip on the liner that was to take us to Africa.

I was so excited, I'd never sailed on such a huge ship before. The weather was warm and sunny, and the sea was calm until we reached the Bay of Biscay where a wild storm rocked even that big ship . . . and Gerald was sea sick . . . again.

For three days, he was sick . . .

Of course, secretly, I reveled in the storm. I was never sea sick, and I had always loved the bleak weather of the Yorkshire moors where I had grown up. But it was hardly conducive to a honeymoon atmosphere.

Finally, the sun came out, the sea became calm. Gerald began to feel better, and since the ship's crew had now opened the swimming pool, he decided we should take an early morning dip. Seeing nobody else in the water, I happily dived in.

Oh dear.

I hadn't noticed the small child swimming along the bottom with a snorkel.

I landed on top of it . . . its sharp edge went right into my lip. What a mess. My mouth swelled up and it certainly couldn't bare being touched. So much for expectations of returning to newly wedded bliss.

But that's not the end of my honeymoon saga.

On the last day of our cruise by which time my lip was better, Gerald and I entered the Greasy Pole competition in the final swimming gala.

In turn, each participant had to slide along this pole, which was placed across the pool, and try to knock an opponent into the water. A large, blown up inner tube was the weapon to be used to accomplish this.

Gerald was knocked out early, but I managed to reach the finals. A tall, burly Swede was waiting for me, grinning, ready for the kill.

I wobbled my way to meet him, the tube by now just as greasy as the slippery pole.

We swung away at each other; little effect; the audience yelled in glee.

Suddenly, as I took a more energetic swing, the tube flew out of my hand. Trying to grab it, I continued my swing, closing my fingers over empty air as I tried to make contact.

And make contact I did . . . with the chin of that burly Swede.

Off the pole he plunged, then came up gasping for air.

Laughing, he yelled, "Thank God I'm not Mr. Nugent!"

FROGS AND DOGS

The ship docked, our car was unloaded, and we began our journey up country to the little town of Dunkwa over a hundred miles from the coast. This was where we were to live for the next two years.

Of course, I was excited and fascinated by all I saw. Natives carrying huge loads on their heads. Rickety lorries overloaded, with extraordinary mottos emblazoned on the front. I remember one was 'God will save us.' By the appearance of the vehicle, it looked as if it needed all the help it could get.

Much of that road was through dark jungle with tall trees blocking out the sun. Beneath them were plants with enormous leaves: elephant's ears. I wondered if I would see a real elephant, but of course not; they were indigenous to East Africa, I was told. All I saw of animal life on that trip were monkeys.

The journey was long and exhausting, for the road became just a rough, bumpy track across the red laterite earth.

It was dark by the time we reached Dunkwa. At last we stopped.

Now Gerald had told me nothing of what I should expect. Nor did he tell me just what was the building in front of which he had parked the car.

It was small, gray, built of cinderblocks, about the size of a single garage, with no garden or welcoming decoration at all, just tall, overshadowing bushes. Dear God, I thought. Was this where we were to live?

My husband laughed at the horror on my face as he unlocked the door.

"It's all right. This is just the rest house. We'll be going to our home tomorrow. The man who temporarily replaced me will have left by then."

Wretched husband. He should have warned me. I went inside and looked dubiously at the concrete floor, and the two beds hung with mosquito netting. I discovered the mattresses were of straw and the supporting frameworks were crisscrossed rope. I suppose my expression was not one of pleasure.

Taking pity on me, Gerald suggested I have a bath. That would make me feel better.

33

Bath? Yes, there was a bath. It was made of moulded concrete, just like the floor. Rough concrete. As I peered over its edge, I found myself looking into the eyes of a very large frog!

Now this was too much. I ran back to that mosquito shrouded bed.

As I climbed in I heard the sound of beating drums. My husband has so many times laughed as he tells of my fearful comments. "Are the natives friendly?"

Not surprising, I cried myself to sleep.

Next morning I woke to bright sunlight and the cacophony of sound of chattering monkeys. As I looked out the window, I saw the glorious reds and purples of the bougainvillea, which I had seen as dark, gruesome masses the night before; suddenly, the world seemed a better place, it was time to go home.

We drove up the long, winding driveway to the top of the hill where our house sat in splendid isolation. A beautiful house; a spacious bungalow surrounded by gardens and orchards. I mentally forgave my husband for teasing me last night.

But now I was in for another shock. There, lined up in front of the entrance, were seven immaculately dressed servants. Yes. Seven.

Gerald led me forward and introduced them. They greeted my husband with delighted pleasure . . . and bowed politely to me. (I discovered later they were not too happy to have a Madam in charge now.)

I met the cook, the bearer, the small boy, the gardener, the wash man, the chokadah (night watchman), and the driver. Good heavens! What on earth was I to do with them all? Over the next few weeks I discovered why I was not particularly welcome. They had been robbing 'Massa' blind.

When Gerald gave me my housekeeping, he very carefully explained that I was to count the items of food such as the number of rashers in a pound of bacon. (I even discovered there were about a hundred lumps of sugar in a box.) I was told to be careful with that money, for the servants were not above helping themselves. Of course I was careful. I was going to be the best housekeeper . . .

At the end of the month, I found I had only spent about half what I had been given.

Of course, while only Gerald had lived in that house, the servants had not stolen those counted purchases, they knew about them . . . they had just stolen from everything else.

They soon realized that 'Madam' had caught on,

A little later, the cook came to Gerald.

"Either Madam go, or I go."

He was quite surprised when my husband chose me to stay; after all, women who gave 'palaver' (trouble) were worthless . . . weren't they?

My husband had a dog, a white bull terrier. A friend had looked after him until Gerald came back . . . with a wife.

Nero never liked me. He had been used to sleeping on the bed and didn't see why he should be shut out of the bedroom just because I had arrived. It became a sort of armed neutrality.

Then the poor animal became sick. He developed a large cyst under his chin. We had no local vet, and our doctor couldn't risk treatment less he were bitten. The only relief Nero could find was to put his chin on the cool S bend of the toilet. Now this caused no problem for Gerald, but for me, that was a different matter. During the day, when my husband was at work, I visited our neighbors much more often than usual!

Eventually, we had to have Nero shot, for he was suffering so much. That was a sad day for Gerald, but I was quietly grateful to have again the use of our only toilet.

AN AFRICAN WEDDING

"How would you like to go to a real African wedding?" My husband stood on the veranda of our bungalow looking at an invitation that had just come in the morning mail. "Oh, yes. Of course, I want to go!"

I, a new bride, had been in West Africa for about a couple of months and was still wide eyed at the charm and laughter on the faces of the locals.

"Now, don't be too hasty, I'm not really sure we're expected to attend; the invitation is from my clerk of works, and I think all he wants is a nice present." Gerald sounded dubious; I realized that my eagerness was causing him to regret telling me about the wedding.

"Oh, please. It'll be exciting. Surely they'll love it if the boss comes." I had visions of tribal dancing, flickering firelight, machetes and shields; I had seen too many Tarzan films!

"Well . . . " My husband grinned at my enthusiasm.

"We'll buy him a really lovely present. How about a bedside lamp, or a set of cutlery?" My knowledge of African life was still somewhat sketchy. My husband seemed even more amused.

"Perhaps he might like a more practical piece of furniture." New husbands can be delightfully tolerant. And so a reply of acceptance was sent off and a set of small tables purchased.

Eventually, the great day arrived. Gerald wore a formal suit instead of his usual tropical whites, and I wore my wedding going-away dress, completing the outfit with a large pink hat. Feeling quite smart, determined to show our respect for the bride and groom, we drove to the little church on the far side of town. We parked our car and walked to the front entrance. The milling crowd parted to allow us through. The men were clad in Kenti cloths thrown over their shoulders like Roman senators, and the women wore bright, floor-length, Mammy-cloth dresses, such a kaleidoscope of vivid colors.

We were escorted to the front of the church to two enormous chairs; heaven knows from where they had got them.

Gerald whispered to me, a twinkle in his eyes, "I told you we weren't expected to come." He turned his head. "Look around. We're the only whites."

But nothing ventured, nothing won, or something like that. I lifted my head and grinned back. I was determined to enjoy myself.

By the time the ceremony was due to begin, the whole building was crowded. The open windows had people hanging over the sills, determined to get a view of the proceedings—though I realized that we were as much the center of attraction as the groom and best man who were waiting at the altar, each dressed in formal English suits, just like my husband. I began to feel a little uncomfortable as the thought occurred to me that these were not their normal style of wear. I hated to think that their choice was in deference to the boss.

But I soon forgot this as a bubble of laughter began to rise in my throat. Each man was wearing one glove, on opposite hands; a smart, brand-new, white glove. I wondered where they had got the idea that only one was necessary. Or was it that the exchequer could not rise to two pairs of gloves? The thought quelled my amusement, though only a little. Thank goodness the music soon started, and I was able to cough into my handkerchief to hide my threatened giggles. I could feel Gerald's shoulders shake as he, too, put his hand to his mouth and cleared his throat.

Oh, dear, I thought. I just hope we don't disgrace ourselves. It's so hard in church to stop the laughter once it starts.

The music increased and the whole congregation turned to watch the bride walk down the aisle on the arm of her father,.

Everyone, smiled and cheered happily, and I looked in startled amazement. The girl was resplendent in an enormous white bridal gown. It needed to be enormous, for she was at least eight and a half months pregnant. Gerald's snort was lost in the noise, thank goodness, and I managed to close my mouth before my expression of high glee at the ludicrousness of the picture erupted into laughter. I would not have offended them for the worlds, but whatever else I expected at that wedding, certainly not this.

Fascinated, I watched the bride waddle down to the altar and eventually kneel, with much puffing and blowing, rather like a small whale, in front of the rather bleary-eyed minister.

So the ceremony began.

"Dearly beloved brethren . . ." We settled back. The congregation was quiet. Expecting a long peroration on the sanctity of marriage, my mind wandered. I watched the dancing motes of dust quiver in the bright, morning sunlight. The day was hot and I was beginning to wilt.

Suddenly, startled, I began to pay closer attention. "You must lust," the minister's voice boomed out; "you must lust only for each other." Now this really was too much. Quite obviously, the lusting had been well satisfied. "Put away all carnal thoughts of others, and lust only for each other."

37

The dear man, obviously far from sober after the previous evening's bachelor party, which, apparently, had gone on most of the night, was at least three sheets to the wind. But he was determined to make sure his message was clear. "Lusting after others is of the Devil!"

I concentrated on my eyelids, keeping them wide open, and controlling the muscles of my face; it was essential I didn't laugh. After all, the congregation seemed fully appreciative of the sentiment. "Amen. Amen." they solemnly agreed.

Gerald had bowed his head, apparently praying!

Next came the exchanging of vows and the wedding ring. I was glad of the change of pace. I didn't think my aching sides could take much more.

The bride was wearing a pair of long, white gloves, the left one of which had to be removed. Her father, who was still standing beside her, turned to help her.

Carefully, he first unfastened something that was holding the glove in place, then he stuck the object in the lapel of his jacket. When he had peeled off the glove and turned back to face the minister, I was able to see what it was. There in all its glory was a large, obviously brand-new, baby's diaper pin.

Gerald and I clasped each other's hand as tightly as we could. "Prepared for any sudden emergency, I presume." Gerald muttered to me.

Oh dear. It was so hard not to laugh. but we knew we must not, it would be so rude.

The ceremony complete, we all repaired to the local football field where the reception was to be held. Gerald and I were led to a covered dais next to the platform where sat the bride and groom. A large sheet of paper was given to us on which was written the order of proceedings. Not paying it too much attention, we at last felt able to relax our carefully schooled faces.

But our laughter was not over.

Someone came to ask us what we would like to drink. Whisky or Coca-Cola. My husband said the first, thank you; and I, the second.

A tray eventually was placed on our table. Two neat, hand embroidered napkins, a bottle of Coca-Cola, and a large bottle of Scotch . . . but no glasses. Grinning at the discomfort of my husband, I took the napkin and carefully wiped the mouth of my Cola bottle.

"Cheers." I said.

With a shrug of his shoulders, he grinned back.

"Cheers to you, too." He lifted the whisky bottle and did the same. "When in Rome," he laughed as he took a swig. Now this was hardly a morning drink, and neat whisky is extremely potent. Spluttering, it took him a minute to join in my laughter.

But he had the last laugh that afternoon.

The reception continued with gifts brought to the bride and groom, and we watched the happy smiles.

Our eyes had been wandering over the faces of the assembled guests, for I was fascinated by the kaleidoscope of colors. Gradually we became aware that the people were no longer looking at the bride and groom, but at us. More specifically, at me. Everyone was now silent.

Bewildered, I looked at Gerald, then we both looked at our paper on which was written the order of proceedings.

'Presentation of the Gifts.' That seemed to be finished. What was next?

'Cutting of the Cake. By Mrs. Nugent.'

Highly amused, Gerald gave me a shove. "You'd better go do it," he whispered. "They might lynch you if you don't."

Now this wasn't funny. I had no idea what I was supposed to do. Leaving our dais, I slowly moved to the table on which stood a tiered, white-iced, wedding cake. Nobody came to instruct me. The whole congregation just sat and looked at me.

I looked at the cake, and it looked back at me.

The table held only one other item. The largest scimitar I had ever seen. It looked more like an executioner's sword than a cake knife. And that, I was told afterwards, was just what it was.

I gulped and reached my hand to lift it. It barely moved in my tentative clasp. Finally, in desperation, I put both hands around the handle and heaved.

It wavered in the air as I looked at that poor cake. Then squelch. That scimitar sliced through that icing as if it were butter.

For a moment, I stood there, not daring to attempt to lift the sword unless the whole cake went flying across the field.

Suddenly, the whole crowd erupted into cheers, and the hefty groom, beaming his smiles, came to relieve me.

I scuttled back to my place on the dais to be greeted by my wretched husband who was in paroxysms of mirth.

"I really thought you were going to drop that thing on your toe," he laughed. "That'll teach you to be more careful about the invitations you accept!"

But the laughter was not over yet, and I had other lessons to learn.

Our invitation included a wedding breakfast that was to be held the following evening at the groom's house. Gerald only had a vague idea where that was, for the village where his clerk of works lived had no conventional street signs; the locals usually just plonked down their huts where the mood took them.

Eventually, we found the place, for all the villagers were crowded around the outside, peering through the open, square holes, which were the African equivalent of windows. When I went inside, I realized just how silly I had been with my suggestions of bedside lamps and cutlery. There were two rooms, and the floors were beaten-down earth. Our nest of tables had been given pride of place beside a rickety arm chair. The only other pieces of furniture were trestle tables, around which were metal chairs, apparently borrowed from the office.

The bride and groom, with their family guests, were waiting to greet us, and they seated us at a table. I sat next to the bride and was pleased to discover that she was a teacher at the local village school. Her English was quite good and we chattered about her life. Gerald was at the other side of the table so was not listening to our conversation.

Of course, there was one question I was dying to ask, but I knew my husband would not approve, so lowering my voice, I began to talk about the baby. She told me what she would call it if it were a boy, and how all her family would help her look after the child so she could go back to teaching. But she still did not tell me what I wanted to know. Finally, I could stand it no longer.

"Why didn't you marry sooner?" I blurted out. "Er . . . you won't have much time for a honeymoon." I remember blushing; not only because I was embarrassed, but because I knew Gerald would be angry with me for intruding in private matters.

The bride laughed. "Oh, your ideas are so different from ours. In our country, a good man will not waste himself on a barren woman, or one who cannot carry a child."

Stunned, I tried to assimilate this totally different idea. All my high moral principles, which had been dinned into me since childhood, suddenly seemed narrow. And yet, she was a Christian woman, teaching at a Christian school.

But the practicality of the African's view of life was not something I could discount. These people love children, and want many of them. A man's pride is lessened if he cannot have sons. I felt humbled as I swallowed my mental criticism.

Conversation became general and the meal was served. What happened next should have caused even more mirth for Gerald and me, but now I learned a more beautiful lesson.

Plates were brought to each place and forks were handed to us. I looked down at my food in surprise. Heinz potato salad. I knew it was Heinz because that was the only canned type the local store sold. It wasn't my favorite food, so I ate just a polite amount, wanting to save space for the wonderfully flavorsome African curry for which Ghana is famous.

Our plates were removed and fresh ones brought. This time we were served Heinz baked beans . . . and Heinz potato salad.

Then came the next dish. Heinz spaghetti . . . and potato salad. And the next; Heinz beef stew . . . and potato salad. We actually had seven different servings, each with Heinz potato salad.

By now, Gerald and I should have been doubled up with mirth at our host's crude effort to emulate the boss's dining table. But no. We both felt extraordinarily humbled. How many of us would pay such honor to our guests to give them only what was their type of food? We are too smug, believing that our western culture is definitely supreme.

I felt ashamed of my superficial laughter, at my critical amusement during the wedding ceremony, and at my condescension over no glasses for our Coca-Cola and whiskey.

That weekend I learned to open my mind, to try to understand another culture, and to appreciate the gentle kindness of these wonderful people.

THE WITCH DOCTOR

Our western scientific knowledge is far greater than that of a little local man in the depths of the African Jungle. At least, that was what I thought.

How ignorant and complacent can a new arrival in that continent be?

Gerald, as District Engineer in the little town of Dunkwa, was responsible for an area of about 5,000 square miles, and a major project he was planning was a new road linking this town to the big city, Kumasi.

When the surveying was complete, the first clearing of the forest began. All the work was to be done by local labor, and careful time schedules were kept so that a bridge across a small river some miles along the route could be built during the dry season.

At least, that was the intention.

Now dry season in West Africa means just that. A season of no rain. It's a time of hot, parched months when the dusty, easterly Harmattan winds blow down from the Sahara, usually from November to March. A haze of tiny sand particles blocks out the sun, uncomfortable for breathing, but the land is cooler, and the rivers and streams dry up.

This, obviously, was the best time to build the bridge, and construction should have been straight forward. That is, if nothing slowed down the work. After all, it was just a small bridge over a small river. It was really a fairly simple job . . . if Mother Nature co-operated.

No such luck! The vagaries of most unusual weather soon put paid to my husband's time schedule.

At the beginning of that dry season, Gerald was supervising the installation of the necessary coffer dam so the remaining water in the river could be diverted in preparation for concrete piers to be poured. He and his crew were well on time, with future months of no rain to interfere.

Along came a rather ancient local chief, full of curiosity.

"Massa. Road go through my village?" he asked. Obviously, such a road would bring prosperity.

Gerald patiently explained that the shortest route to Kumasi had been chosen. Costs had to be considered.

"Humph! Road no go through my village, big palaver." (A local word for trouble)

The wizened old man stalked away not at all pleased.

Gerald shrugged his shoulders in some sympathy, but the alignment could not be changed and the work continued.

That night, it rained.

But it never rained in the dry season, surely?

It rained with such intensity that when Gerald returned to the site in the morning, the coffer dam had been washed away. The weeks' work had been wasted.

He was met by the same old man who danced up and down in glee.

"See, Massa. I tell you big palaver. Now road go through my village?"

Inevitably the same negative answer. Of course it couldn't. This had been just a freak storm . . . hadn't it?

Frustrated by the damage, but determined to get that bridge built on time, the men began to construct another coffer dam.

A week later, the now-dry river bed was again ready for the concrete piers to be poured.

Along came the old man once more.

"Massa. Road go through my village?"

He was informed again that it was impossible. The shortest distance between two places, etc., etc. Irritated and probably not too politely, Gerald urged him to leave.

"Road no go through my village, big palaver," was the old man's parting shot as he stalked off indignantly.

That night it rained.

Yes, just as heavily as before. But this never happened in the dry season. Certainly not twice. . . . Strange.

Of course, the new coffer dam was washed away and work was back to square one.

The next morning, again the old man returned.

By this time, the workers were restless. The Africans are an immensely superstitious people. They watched as the little man, chest puffed out, marched up to Gerald.

"See. I tell you. Road no go through my village, big pa-laver."

Waving his Juju stick and rattling the shells in the gourds he was carrying, he cursed the whole project in his local language. Probably cursed Gerald, too.

Over the next weeks, work was doubled, extra staff were brought in, for that bridge had to be finished before the end of the dry season. Surely there could be no more rain.

But there was. Again it poured and poured. And again, when Gerald returned to the site, the old man was there, as usual, grinning all over his face. He knew he had won.

... Now, when you drive from Dunkwa to Kumasi, much of the road is straight; but there is a small kink by a bridge where a bend takes you at least a mile out of the original planned direction before returning to the original line.

It goes through a village ...

That Juju man must have long sat under his Tamarind tree enjoying his great power, much respected by his people. After all, he had got the better of the great white master!

Of course I should end the story there leaving you wondering about the mysterious magic of deep, dark Africa.

But there's a much more prosaic explanation.

Those natives, who had never read a book on meteorology, understood and, no doubt, could smell when the rains were coming.

Good psychologist, that witch doctor. If one knows more than does someone else, and one chooses the right moment ...

And that wily old soul knew just how to manipulate. He so frightened the workmen that they downed tools and refused to continue with that wretched bridge until he got his way.

But it really was a most unusual dry season. Maybe there was a little magic after all. I've always wondered ...

THE DURBAR

In March 1957, when Ghana became independent, a durbar was held in Dunkwa. The chiefs and their retinue traveled from as far away as the Sahara to celebrate the momentous occasion.

A quite extraordinary day. The locals really thought the streets that morning would be paved with gold. Not so. Graft and greed among the new leaders eventually brought disillusionment. Indeed, years later when we were leaving, our Ghanian driver asked Gerald who would be his next master. When told, he made one harsh comment and walked out of Gerald's office.

"I no work for black man!" There had been so much raping of the country's wealth, and so many who opposed the government had disappeared. No wonder people were disillusioned.

But on that day of independence, everyone was happy.

In Dunkwa where we were living, the local football field had been commandeered. A wide, covered platform had been set up for the District Commissioner to whom all the tribes would pay homage. I have a film of the event and still find it hard to believe the noise, the color, the pomp and circumstance of the long line of chiefs from as far north as the Sahara, and as far south as Nigeria.

Tall, stately Hauser Arabs came with long, proud strides, clad in voluminous cloaks, some the deep navy blue with matching turban, part of which was dragged across their faces leaving only their kohled eyes visible. Others wore vivid, flamboyant robes, and many had long beards and carefully curled mustaches. All wore those heavy, loosely wrapped yards of cloth on their heads; some sort of blanket for the bitterly cold desert nights, so I was told.

The wealthy Ghanian chiefs wore brilliantly colored Kenti cloths, draped as Roman togas over crisp, white, short-sleeved shirts. These togas would often be many years old, for they never wore out and were handed down from father to son. The poorer men wore yards of cheaper material, but still draped it toga-like. There is a myth that the lost Roman legions, almost two thousand years ago, found their way across the Sahara to the equatorial forests of West Africa; hence, the draped fashion of Ghanian clothing. One of the symbols the tribal leaders of this people carry on a highly decorated pole is of an eagle . . . the same as did those lost Romans. Hmm. Perhaps their journey is not a myth.

These chiefs all came with their entourage. Their importance was expressed not only by the number of people in their group, but

45

more startlingly, by the size of their umbrellas. Apparently, one of the old photos of Queen Victoria, 'The Great White Queen', showed her carrying a parasol.

These chiefs were determined to emulate Her Majesty and show just how important they were. Bigger and better was the theme! Some were as wide as ten feet across, and the unlucky bearers had to waft them up and down over their masters creating a breeze to keep them cool.

Many had been made in London; rich velvets, vividly printed drapery fabric in every color under the sun, all with silk tassels that danced. Who knows how old those umbrellas were?

The Denkyirahene, the most important chief, arrived with, of course, the biggest umbrella. Then after him came his queen. She was carried in on a skin-covered stretcher. I was surprised to see that she was a small, quite young woman, who was being treated with great reverence and respect. I discovered that once she produced sons she became more important than the present chief. Why? Because she selects the next chief. After all, only the mother can be sure who is the father!

Of course, we had our share of witch doctors daubed with white clay and adorned with multi-colored feathers. Most of them seemed to be as tight as coots, but by the end of the day, so did everyone else.

And jangling through it all was the ghastly cacophony of the drums. Not to be out done, those with no drum had brought their goats. Each group sang their tribal songs, determined to be louder and less melodious than their neighbor.

The noise, the dust, the wild dancing, a world that we will never see again.

At the end was a sad moment as the British flag was slowly lowered, then the Ghanian flag joyfully raised. Little did those people know that their new government would not be as benevolent as their old. And little did those chiefs realize how their authority was going to be minimized under the government of Kwami Nkrumah. A famous present day proponent of the restoration of chieftainship has said, "They were Kings or Emperors who commanded political power and executed justice, were masters and guardians of the treasures of knowledge, wisdom and culture accumulated over thousands of years."

But it was a bewildering, wonderful day; even a somewhat frightening one, for I was not too sure lest all those excited people might not decide to get rid of the local colonial rulers right then!

ANTS

In retrospect, the mind pictures we retain from the past are hilarious, even ludicrous, but at the time, one event was not so amusing.

This particular evening, I was holding a dinner party. It was one of my first as a new wife in Africa and everything had to be just so. Guests were the District Commissioner, the local doctor, the managers of various companies, all with their wives. I was determined everything should go well and that my husband would be proud of me.

Of course, I was nervous, but I had checked everything repeatedly. The house was immaculate, the flowers sweet-smelling and profuse; I had a new dress, and dinner was all ready to be served.

Then began a ghastly fiasco.

Kwaku, our cook, and the bearer, came tearing from the kitchen into the living room where we all sat having pre-dinner drinks. They were carrying burning newspapers.

They threw them over the veranda and, screaming as they ran, rushed back into the kitchen for buckets of flaming fuel they had somehow managed to drag from the wood-burning stove.

Our guests jumped to their feet, the men ready to grab the apparently mad servants.

Then we deciphered the words.

"The ants. The ants go come."

The District Commissioner, a Ghanian, was the only one who understood the danger we were in. He yelled to us, "Help them, Get more paper, anything that will burn. We need fire, as much as possible."

I thought the world had gone mad. What were a few ants?

The fear in his voice galvanized us into action. Windows throughout the house were slammed shut, and all the doors except the one onto the veranda. We women tore up magazines, the men grabbed bundles of split wood from the kitchen, others dragged books from the shelves. We frantically relayed ourselves into a team, throwing more material over the wall until the spiral of flames spread all along the edge of the house.

Through the crackle of the flames and the noise of our own voices and rushing feet, we became aware of another strange sound, almost like the swish of the brushes on a drum. At first, it was faint, a steady, low hum; then it increased as the ants came.

47

Red fire ants. An army of them. Millions, billions, who knows?

In the glow of the flames, we could see this vast black-brown carpet move steadily past the house. Thank God we were only on the edge of their inexorable march, for if their route had been just yards nearer, our puny efforts to keep them out would have been useless. Of course, many got in and attacked us. We tried to slap them away, but they bit so hard that we had to break off their bodies leaving their tenacious jaws still clinging.

But still we managed to keep the fire burning.

For almost two hours we fought those ants.

Then, gradually, that weird drumming faded. The army had passed, and the night was silent.

It was like waking from a nightmare.

What? Where? How? Why? We looked at each other in exhausted bewilderment. Such a short time ago we had been sitting in pleasant peaceful contentment.

And now?

We were smothered in dust and ash, filthy from smoke and still-floating debris from the dying embers. The living room was equally dirty: a wreck of the pristine elegance of my intended dinner party. We collapsed onto chairs: it seemed silly to worry that they, too, were covered in the same grey-black soot.

Our faithful Kwaku, just as exhausted as we were, brought us drinks. Oh, so welcome. We needed them to sooth our parched throats. It was then he told us how he had known that the ants were coming. We had been chattering away and had not been aware of a change in the night. Normally, there would be a cacophony of sound, animals, birds, all contributing to a usual African evening.

Kwaku had stepped out of his kitchen for a moment and had become aware of silence. Utter silence. Then he had heard the faint distant hum, a sound Africans dreaded. The sound of marching ants.

We were in the middle of an unusually dry season: this would happen perhaps once in a decade when the ants would seek water. They would join in one vast army eating everything in their path, be it plant life, animal or human . . . and our house was on the edge of the forest, in almost direct line with the river at the bottom of the hill.

We shuddered as the District Commissioner explained, but the sheer relief of knowing there was no more danger, that our ordeal was really over, brought relaxation, and with it, humor.

First one would chuckle, noticing the raccoon-like circles of black grime around eyes, then another, until we were all laughing, obviously an almost hysterical reaction.

But what else could we do? There was certainly no point in bemoaning anything so trivial as a spoiled dinner party. Even to this day I can remember the change from our elegance sophistication to a group of hobo tramps. There's nothing like a cataclysmic event to make you realize just how valuable is the wonderful gift of humor.

But when the following morning I looked out at the direction from which the ants had come, I did not laugh.

Bare, leafless trees in a width of about thirty yards stretched back into the forest, looking as if a tornado had striped their branches. Eerie, awe inspiring, that those inch-long insects had such power and voracious might when banded together.

I learned later that any small animals in their path would have been devoured in seconds. Nonchalantly, the District Commissioner told me that it would take the ants only a few minutes to eat a cow.

Maybe a human being would last for half that time . . .

JAN VAN BEUKERING

Van B, as we affectionately called him, was our doctor in Dunkwa. He was a great bear of a man, tough, but so kind. His wife was not with him this tour; their sons were in high school, so she had stayed back home in Holland. He missed them, of course, so in the evenings he often came over to visit us and we played bridge. He was quite a demon at the game and invariably won.

"Gott verdammt!" was a favorite saying of his, mostly a joke, but one evening, he told us a story of endurance where God had so nearly damned his family's future. He usually didn't talk about his past, but this particular evening I think he had become maudlin with one drink too many.

1939, he was in the Dutch East Indies with his wife and baby son where he was practicing medicine in one of the big cities.

Frequently, he would make a trip up country to the tribes living deep in the jungle. They had little or no contact with so-called civilization and had no available medical help.

Some times, there would be deep machete wounds that needed stitching. Always curious, he wondered why they never went septic, for usually the natives covered the damaged area with leaves, apparently any leaves. Thinking they must have some healing properties, he took some of them back down to his lab, washed them clean and examined them. Nothing. Just ordinary leaves. He was a busy man, so he forgot about them.

Then the Japanese came.

All the whites were herded into various prison camps, the men in separate ones from the women and children.

Now followed long years of misery. The men had no idea if their families lived or died. All they could do was hope. Between starvation, beatings and dysentery, so many of the men were constantly ill and very weak

Van B was the only doctor in his camp and he told us of having to 'play God'—his own words—by deciding who should live or die. This is when Van B learned to play bridge. Yes: the card game we were playing that evening. It took the prisoners' minds off their suffering.

But more than that, they played for grains of rice, virtually the only food the Japanese gave them. Usually, Van B would win; Then he would decide to whom he should give those grains. (It was his job to supervise the food distribution.) He'd decide who had the best chance of survival.

I have wondered since how deeply was the guilt he must have felt. Cold-bloodedly having to decide a man's life or death must have been almost unendurable for a man who lived by his Hippocratic oath.

I remember that evening sitting there ignoring my cards, quite shaken by the picture Van B had drawn. Perhaps aware that he was not exactly being a good guest and had depressed us too much, he changed from his somber story to one of wry humor.

"Toward the end of the war when the Japanese were on the run, American planes flew over dropping food and medical supplies. This was when I discovered what a dolt I had been. Remember those leaves I told you about?"

Apparently among the various boxes were parcels of a new medicine Van B had never heard of. With it came instructions and its history. It was called penicillin, and it came from a blue mold, which had been purified in 1940 by Sir Alexander Fleming who coined its name.

"Blue mold! That was on those leaves I had washed so carefully. Gott verdammt, I could have invented the stuff!"

He had a wonderful, deep laugh, and enjoyed the end of his story as much as we did.

When he returned to Holland, he bought a house boat on one of the canals and called it, what else? 'The Sir Alexander Fleming'.

Another evening, Van B told us something of the end of those imprisoned years in Sumatra. This time he glossed over the misery.

When they were released from the camps, the families were reunited . . . those who still survived. Not only did he find his wife and son, but he discovered his family had expanded.

Apparently, unknown to either him or his wife, she had been pregnant when they were captured, so now they had a second son.

But there was more to the story. Another wife, also pregnant, had given birth almost at the same time. Sadly, she had died.

Van B's wife could not endure to see that child follow its mother, so she breast fed it with her own baby for two full years. How she and those three children had managed to survive those six years had been little short of a miracle.

"Gott verdammt, those bloody Japanese! But we beat them in the end. We Dutch, we never gave up."

Typical, proud, tough comment of our friend, Van B.

51

KATHERINE

We met some extraordinary people in our travels.

. . . People like Sir Arku Korsah, a brilliant lawyer who was the first black chief justice. He became Ghana's representative to the United Nations.

. . . Brezhnev, eventual General Secretary of the USSR, who had the biggest hands I have ever seen.

. . . Marshal Tito, and his sailors in the Yugoslav navy who told me they had a partiality for chubby women. That night on board their ship, I think I danced more than at most cocktail party, and got pinched far more, too.

. . . The King of Nepal who gave a party where all his guests had to chase ducks. I never did know why?

. . . The Australian Ambassador to Turkey at whose table I got violently sick with food poisoning.

. . . The Chief of the Ibo tribe who ruled over more than five million people in Nigeria. He continuously waved his fly swat over me to keep the mosquitos away. Very thoughtful, I'm sure, but the swishing feathers kept getting in my eyes.

. . . A remarkably handsome, wealthy Parsee who each year went to Italy for his hand-made shoes, to Saville Row in England for his tailored suits, to Paris for his shirts, to Switzerland for his watches, and America for his polo gear. I remember wondering where he bought his underwear but was too polite to ask.

They all were quite famous and I was extremely lucky to have had the honor to meet them. True.

But there was one remarkable lady for whom I had an even greater respect and admiration.

When I met her, she must have been about sixty, and it was from her accountant that I heard her story.

Katherine had been orphaned when she was a small child of ten. Usually such a child would have been taken in by the village where she lived, for loss of parents did not mean loss of family. Indeed, many of the tribes don't even have the word for orphan in their vocabulary.

Now Katherine didn't want to remain there, for she was determined to become a Market Mammy. Much of the food trade was in the hands of the women, and every town and village would have rows of small stalls, each in the charge of an enterprising mammy.

This little girl went to the local wholesale trader and asked for one packet of cigarettes, which she would take to the market and sell. She promised to return with payment within a couple of days. I suppose the trader felt sorry for her, so he handed over the packet not expecting to see her again. Two days later, she was back. She had separated the twenty in the pack and sold them for fractionally less than their usual cost.

She now paid the trader half of what she owed and asked for a whole carton.

She sold these the same way, again returning to the trader and paying half of what she owed.

By now, the local men were sneering at Katherine's stupidity and lined up for her under-cost supply.

But Katherine was no fool.

Next, she bought some lump sugar. Do you know there are almost a hundred cubes in a box?

Same deal, same half-payment of her bill.

Next, she added sardines and candles to her little stall.

Of course, her customers were becoming used to dealing with her, so gradually she increased her prices, beginning to make a profit.

All this time, Katherine did not go to school, never learned to read, received no formal instruction in math. Yet without any classroom education, she prospered.

My! How she prospered.

I met her at a cocktail party she was attending with her business managers and her accountant. He was ruefully telling us of the enormous amount of income tax for which the government was pestering her.

Eventually, Katherine bought out the trader from whom she had bought that original packer of cigarettes and cornered the market in most of the general products he supplied. She still could not read or write, though she could recognize words like sugar, sardines and cigarettes. She gradually supplied not only Mammy stalls all up and down the country, but also the major stores.

Fifty years after her early beginning, Katherine was now a multi-millionaire.

From rags to riches with nothing but her own ingenuity and guts. Is it any wonder that I admired her so much?

There's more to the story.

She had four daughters, each of whom had gone to first class British and American Universities. Education had become something of a God to Katherine, and she supported many of the local schools, helping so many girls achieve their dreams.

People like Katherine made me feel ashamed at the way I complacently took for granted my upbringing, but it tickled me how strongly she advocated the importance of education for women, quite indignant that men should presume they were more deserving than their sisters, wives and daughters!

There was another, equally impressive market mammy, Mrs. Jagger.

Ghana at that time was really a matriarchal society, for the women ran many of the local businesses, and Mrs. Jagger was their spokesperson.

One day, the dock workers at Temma Harbor, (all men), went on strike. This was devastating, for all imports and exports went through this harbor.

Negotiations made no progress so, in desperation, the government approached Mrs. Jagger. With absolute assurance, she promised that every one of these men would be back at work in three days.

Sure enough, they were.

Rather red faced, the authorities asked how she had done it. It was hard for them to stomach that a woman could succeed when they hadn't.

"Oh. Quite easy. I merely told the women to 'withhold their favors' until their men went back to work."

Quite hilarious, but don't ever underestimate the power of women!

SPORTS EDUCATION, THE SERIOUS STUFF

I suppose I could have bored you with the years and years of learning, first studying architecture, then education, but as I look back, my major memories are of sport.

Hockey, tennis, swimming, and athletics; I wondered how I would live without them when I left school.

I never had as many trophies as Gerald, but I had a few and was on every team into which I could inveigle my way. I was even Victrix Laudorum at Huddersfield, and I held the record for the long jump at the County Championships: 19ft. 2ins. My father, who had a slightly warped sense of humor, remarked that he was not surprised. I always did leap farther than most people . . . usually into trouble!

This love of sports I have continued, expanding it through our children. Wherever we have lived in the States, I have run programs involving as many local kids as I could coerce.

I even took ninety children skiing, once. I must have been crazy! Luckily, we all came home with only minor bruises.

But before I married and had any children of my own, my sporting activities were totally self-centered. I was quite proud of my achievements.

Then I saw Gerald play tennis!

Now that was humbling. Since then I have often said he was the most beautiful player I had ever seen, and I realized my successes were puny in comparison to his international standard; it was a bit deflating to discover that in this area, any prowess I thought I had was decidedly mundane.

But one day I had the chance to get my own back, to show my lord and master that I could beat him at something.

We had been living in Dunkwa for over a year, and a few of us expatriates decided we would get up a hockey game. I had no doubt about my ability there.

I badgered Gerald into agreeing to play, though he said I would have to teach him, particularly how to handle this strange, curved stick.

Oh, I liked the sound of this, and with a delightful sense of superiority, I rather smugly went through the elementary procedures.

"Where shall I play?" he humble asked.

"Somewhere toward the back." I thought he couldn't do much harm there.

The game started.

The opposition won the ball and proceeded to take it down the field, right toward Gerald. With a grin on his face and total assurance, he caught it on his stick and dribbled his way past everyone, all the way to the net and scored a goal.

When I wiped the egg off my face, I stuttered, "You've played hockey before?"

"Yes," he replied. "The last match I played was for England against Germany."

The wretched man. He couldn't restrain his laughter; he had known I was hoping to show him that there really was some sport at which I was better.

No such luck!

I could have killed him!

Only much later did I get my own back.

I discovered golf.

Eventually, Gerald taught me how to play, though it took me a couple of years to get the hang of the game, which I played almost every day in Africa.

Finally, I beat him. This was a red-letter day for me.

Yet even then I didn't get the satisfaction of one-up-man-ship.

Of course, next time we played I lost, as usual.

But nothing daunted, I persisted, and eventually I could beat him on a regular basis. In more recent years, we have played for a million dollars a match! Mainly lighthearted competition, but as I chalked up those millions—only in fun, of course—they did feel good.

Gerald never minded being beaten by me; indeed, praised what little ability I had. But there was one occasion when he was furious at another activity where I had some success.

When we were living in Accra, I became involved in the British Council Dramatic Society. I had always loved acting and had taken courses in drama at college. We were to put on Shakespeare's 'Twelfth Night' for the local schools and university. I was the producer.

I loved it, but I became so involved that almost every evening for three months I was down at the theater.

Guiltily, I became aware that Gerald's patience was beginning to wear thin.

One day, the leading man came to our house for something or other. He rang the bell, and Gerald opened the door.

"Oh. You must be Mrs. Nugent's husband," was the greeting. I cringed.

Nobody, but nobody refers to his lordship in that manner. 'Mrs. Nugent's husband' indeed! Unwittingly, he had designated Gerald as the less importance member of our marriage.

Oh dear. When that young man left, I received a furious blast.

"If you want to remain married to me, this is the last production in which you will be involved!"

And that was the end of my career in the theater, particularly as very soon after, I discovered I was pregnant with Rachel.

Now this soon-to-be production was much more acceptable to my happier husband.

. . . and an activity in which he agreed I should excel.

A TROPICAL DISEASE

Before we moved to Accra, we spent a year in Takoradi on the coast. Our house was on the rocky shore about a couple of hundred yards from the Atlantic Ocean. The pounding of the waves and the constant spray were permanent parts of our life; a combination of music and moisture very welcome in that hot climate.

Each evening, I took baby Greg down to the swimming pool at the club. He loved it; he'd kick his chubby little legs in great glee and soon had a healthy tan.

But oh dear, that healthy look didn't last. I learned a grim lesson about tropical diseases.

One day I noticed a little blister behind Greg's ear. Not too concerned, I put on some ointment. Surely it would go away.

The next day, there was another . . . and another.

These blisters swelled up, grew bigger, became hard, just like large carbuncles. I took the poor, uncomfortable little chap to the various local doctors, but none of them could isolate the germ that must be responsible. Every antibiotic available was tried; no success.

Those horrid boils grew so large and were so painful that each morning I had to take a razor and slice open each one and remove the solid, septic lump. Greg would almost sigh in relief as the pressure was relieved. The doctors assured me that he wouldn't feel the cut; otherwise, I couldn't do it, for you can imagine how agonizing it was to slice into ones own child's head.

We lived in Dettol, an antiseptic; indeed, the whole house reeked of it, and for the next few weeks we struggled, none of us getting much sleep, It was agonizing to watch our defenseless baby suffer. I was so frustrated I was almost prepared to visit a local witch doctor; not so bizarre as it might seem, for they had knowledge of local herbs and medicine of which our European doctors knew nothing.

In desperation, I finally decided to change Greg's diet. Our doctors told me not to do so; he needed to keep up his strength. But everything they had done had brought no improvement. If this didn't work, I intended to take him back to England to the School of Tropical Medicine.

Quite why I chose he food I did, I don't know. Call it mother's intuition.

I took him off milk, cereal and his bottled baby food and began to feed him lightly boiled fish, pureed green beans and lemon juice. I remember the poor little soul was so listless that he didn't argue and dutifully swallowed these strangely-flavored foods.

Within five days, no new carbuncles appeared, and the old ones had begun to dry up. By the end of the next week, they had all gone, and Greg was at last sleeping properly. So were we!

Of course, we went no more to the swimming pool as that seemed to be the most likely place from where he had picked up this horrid tropical disease. We weren't going to risk our precious baby.

I have a photo of him on his first birthday when at last he was getting better; his hair was just beginning to grow again. How thin and pale he looked, with dark circles under his eyes.

That was a terrible time, for we so nearly could have lost him, but I never forgot my panacea for that ghastly illness and often reminded us all of my cure.

Yet even out of that near tragedy we eventually found humor. If any of the children were sick, they would groan.

"We're not that bad, we don't need lightly boiled fish, green beans, or sour lemon juice!"

IT'S A SMALL WORLD

Africa is a huge continent: the population is greater than that of the United States, which can fit into the Sahara desert. Even the number of expatriates, as we were called, was considerable. In Accra alone, there were many hundreds.

In 1959, we were home on leave from Africa and decided to take a golfing holiday leaving baby Greg, who was two, with my mother.

It was February, but an unusually mild winter, so each day we went to a new course, played a round of golf, then drove to a hotel in the next town to repeat the same activity. Lovely!

One day, after our game was over, we went into the club house where two dear old biddies were sitting having their pre-dinner gin and tonic—or maybe post-lunch. We joined them at the bar and they asked us where we were from.

"We are home on leave from Africa."

"Oh, we know someone in Africa." Inward groans from us.

"Which part?" we politely asked.

"West Africa," they said.

Now that could encompass an area half the size of Europe, but I was brought up to be polite to strangers. "Oh yes, which part of West Africa?"

"Ghana." (That's about the size of England.) At least, it was the country where we lived. I thought I might as well continue my questions since these old ladies were rather sweet.

"And where in Ghana?"

"A town called Bibiani." Now at this, I pricked up my ears; we knew Bibiani well. It was a gold mining center not very far from Dunkwa.

"These friends of yours, what's their name?"

There could be a slight possibility we might know them. You have to realize that all this time these ladies were showing no surprise at the fact they were talking to people who had come from such a large continent thousands of miles away.

They gave us the name. Both Gerald and I gasped. This was the couple with whom we had spent our last weekend before coming home on leave. Great friends, really special people. What an extraordinary coincidence! No doubt most probably hardly one chance in a million.

But the most amusing ending to the story is that these two ladies showed no surprise at all. Since their Bibiani friends and we came from Africa, of course we would know each other.

. . . Because it really is a small, small, small world!

FOUNTAINS

When we returned from leave, we were transferred to Accra, the capital. Now Gerald's work entailed much closer communication with Kwami Nkrumah, the President of Ghana.

One day the dynamic leader decided he wanted to impress a future visiting dignitary and had a brilliant idea. He had seen spectacular fountains shooting water high into the air in the center of some broad esplanade when he had been touring another country Wonderful! He ordered copies to be delivered immediately . . . but forgot about certain necessary parts.

"Handle it, Nugent," he demanded as he proudly showed off one of these fountains, telling where he wanted them placed along the main road. Of course, his word was law; he didn't care about the logistics.

Gerald was fairly used to the idiosyncrasies of Nkrumah, but even he was stumped how to produce spraying water out of each fountain. Laying pipes was fairly easy since there already were lines that could be tapped into. Power was available, too. So far, so good, but how were these fountains going to be made to work? There had to be some sort of pressure system to create the high jets the President had demanded . . . at regular intervals, of course.

Such equipment had not arrived with the shipment.

Now, Ghana's dynamic, mesmerizing leader, with piercing green eyes usually got what he wanted. "Now, now!" was a typical demand. There was no time to wait for delivery of that missing equipment, so Gerald, refusing to be beaten, used good old British ingenuity.

Large groups of work men tore up the required areas, laid pipes, installed power lines, and put the fountains in position. Shrubbery was planted adjacent, with an empty space in the middle.

Now came Gerald's brainwave. Logical common sense told him it should work, but he certainly crossed his fingers when the water pipes were attached to the ubiquitous toilet.

Yes! A toilet, just the same as we all have in our bathrooms.

Eureka! It worked, just as Gerald had hoped.

As each porcelain water tank filled to the top, the stop cock lifted and opened the down pipe. Then the water flushed with its usual great force.

Presto! A jet rose high into the air from the center of the fountain. Timers were set so that the tanks would flush alternately, and then new piped water would fill them up for the next display.

Fascinating.

The locals were delighted with White Massa's brilliance. More importantly, Kwami Nkrumah was, too.

Gerald breathed a sigh of relief, but wished his new fame was not based on toilets.

RACHEL

Rachel, our older daughter, was such a good baby and would sit placidly looking at the world, sometimes with a tiny frown on her face as she tried to understand its vagaries. I often think this sweetness was a gift from the good Lord who tried to make up for the absolutely ghastly scare we experienced when she was six months old.

Even as I write, I shudder.

We were living in Accra where there was a British school. Each morning, after I had bathed and fed Rachel, I put her in her pram so the nanny could take her for a walk in the cool of the morning. I then went to school and taught until mid day, at which time, when I returned, she would be waking up from her nap ready for lunch.

This particular morning, when I came home, the servants were distraught. "Baby no come home. Baby no come home."

It transpired that the nanny had not returned.

At first, I thought she must have stopped to visit a neighbor who had a baby the same age, quite usual, for the children enjoyed playing together.

No. The servants had checked.

I grabbed the phone and called Gerald.

Screech of brakes when he drove into the compound.

In no time, he called all our friends, then the police, the army, the American Embassy, the British Embassy. This was his beloved daughter and the world must stop to find her.

Which it duly did.

We two drove around the local area asking questions of all we met.

Even in the market, we asked, "You see bruny (white) baby?" The Africans love children and were so concerned for us, spreading the word until the whole population was searching for Rachel.

Backward and forward, we drove. You can imagine our desperate anguish.

It was the month of October, the time of human sacrifice, and only later did Gerald give me the full details of what could have happened. But I did know enough to fear the torture that could be inflicted. I kept saying to myself, "I hope she's dead, I hope she's dead." The idea of her suffering was beyond what I could face.

64

As I look back, I realize I must have been almost unhinged. How could any mother wish her child were dead? But I did. I suppose I was torturing myself in an agony of need to suffer in her place. I don't know. All I do know was that it was a time of unbearable panic. Even today, whenever I hear of kidnapping, I remember the unendurableness of what was so nearly a tragedy.

About 7:30 that evening, we returned yet again to the house to see if there were any news. The driveway was full of cars and army jeeps. Soldiers and policemen surrounded them. Dear God. We rushed up the steps into the living room, dreading what we might find.

Then overwhelming relief. There was the nanny, and she was holding Rachel.

I cared nothing for what had happened and why. I wanted my baby. I pulled her into my arms. With her usual sweet grin, she cooed up at her mother. I was unutterably intensely grateful.

Not so, her father. He was like a wild thing and tore toward the police who were grasping a frightened man cowering next to the nanny. He, as we discovered, was the instigator of the kidnapping. I thought my husband was going to kill him.

It took three policeman to keep Gerald from committing murder. Blazingly angry, he recognized the man as one whom he had fired from work for being a trouble maker, who, no doubt, had intended to wreck vengeance on his master. But how dare he attempt to hurt an innocent child?

When the emotional stress eased, and Gerald had been persuaded to let the man live, we were told just how remarkably lucky we were to have our daughter back, alive and well.

Apparently, one of the policemen, who had been searching the outskirts of Accra, noticed two parallel tire tracks going along a path into the foothills. Wondering if they could be those of Rachel's pram, he followed and eventually caught up with the nanny and the man just before they reached the jungle. There were sacrificial grounds hidden in there, far from civilization. If that policeman had been later, who knows what the ending of the story might have been? A white girl-child was the ideal human sacrifice.

That night, when the police had left, taking their prisoners with them, Gerald and I, with Greg, our four-year-old, hugged, cried, prayed, and loved together our totally happy, uncaring baby. Who knows what she had eaten during those hours away, but it had been just another delightful day as far as she was concerned.

One curious fact I discovered that night, and following nights.

I had expected I would go into traumatic shock . . . reaction to the agony I had endured. But nothing. I slept that night like a log, and the following nights, as well. I never did have any physical reaction.

The body is a marvelous thing. When life is beyond endurance, it shuts down, simply because it can take no more. Of course, it still functions, but it protects us from the unbearable. After that, I no longer went each morning to teach.

THE SCHOOL IN ACCRA

Though I shudder as I remember that day, I still have pleasant memories of the dear little school to which I had gone each morning for three hours. We had ninety students ranging from five years old to twelve, of twenty-one different nationalities. Three hours doesn't seem enough, but we worked those children sufficiently hard that when they returned to their original countries, they had kept up their level of education.

Of course, it was not all grind.

We decided to put on a play including all of them. Tough with the language differences, but perhaps if we had plenty of action for the children . . .

Because my education background included drama, the chore was dumped on my shoulders. I wracked my brains. I needed a theme.

In my class was a particularly delightful child who was from Sierra Leone. He had a high, intelligent forehead and large eyes, which could look as sad as any spaniel if he were trying to cull sympathy from his teacher—such a lugubrious expression he knew would usually make me laugh.

Ha! He gave me a wonderful idea.

'*Old King Cole was a merry . . . no . . . sad old soul.*' What could we do to make him cheerful? An ideal theme.

Oh, how convoluted my story became. We had a prince and a princess, who could not marry unless King Cole was happy—shades of British pantomime—an evil Nanki Poo—shades of the Mikado—and every form of singing, dancing, tumbling and gymnastics of which our students were capable.

One of our friends was a brilliant pianist who was working on her doctorate. I persuaded her to write what turned out to be almost a concerto, with the music of the nursery rhyme, 'Old King Cole' weaving throughout.

The children's parents were delighted with our efforts, and what had, at first, been a rather mad idea, turned into a quite remarkable production. We had national dances in national costumes, songs of other countries, African drummers, we even had two Masai who jumped amazingly high.

And so the night of the performance arrived. The sheer logistics of having everyone in order, seated back stage until it was their

67

turn, could have been a nightmare, but each child was so enthusiastic and waited silently and behaved beautifully.

Then tragedy almost struck. My 'Old King Cole' had flu.

Knowing the show could not go on without him, his worried mother dosed him up with medicine and pushed him onto the stage with a very large handkerchief.

When the curtains were opened, there sat our King, eyes streaming, looking the most unhappy of actors.

Our off-stage group of singers began to sing their mournful dirge . . . "Old King Cole was a sad Old Soul . . .' well punctuated with the large, trumpeting sound of His Majesty blowing his nose.

Of course, the audience loved it; particularly as the more enthusiastic were the children in their attempts to make him smile, the sadder he looked.

Now whether at the end of the last scene, our King Cole was just so relieved that he could leave the stage, or whether he did actually feel more cheerful, I never was sure, but he gave a big beaming smile . . . and the prince and the princess could marry and live happily ever after.

I had another child in one of my classes, Ametowobla, a ten-year-old. Over the years, I have watched for his name in Ghanian politics, for he was the most brilliant child I have ever taught. I say, 'taught,' absurd word: all I could do was guide him. He worked on mature research papers and always was into one encyclopedia or another. But African politics has so often seen the removal of opposition, and Amet's father was against the greed of those in power. I will always wonder . . .

But at that time, we were untouched by the political changes and lived in our little cocoon, creating amusing activities that would combine the capabilities of all those in the school, 'Old King Cole' being only one example, though you can imagine the logistics of co-ordinating dancing, singing, and tumbling; particularly as many of the children spoke very poor English. I felt more like a sergeant major than a drama coach.

Perhaps some of the children still remember. I hope so.

THE QUEEN

It is hard for a nation that has no dynastic heritage to understand the anachronism of the British monarchy. It has no official power; it makes no laws; it dispenses no justice; it dictates no policy; in short, it no longer rules.

And why all those castles? Why so many treasures such as the crown jewels? But they are only held in trust by whoever is the present King or Queen; they truly belong to the nation and are part of the wonderful pomp, ceremony, and heritage of our small island race.

I would not want the job of holding that trust for anything. Sadly, the media tends to highlight the surface of the royal family, describes only the public incidents, particularly if there is any salacious scandal. Yet little is said about the almost unendurable hours of public service, or the sheer exhaustion that comes from them. I know that I could never live up to the Queen's total dedication to her people. All her adult life she has epitomized the true meaning of the word servant, and she has never faltered in that service.

But that is boring stuff and does not sell newspapers. Exaggeration and scandalization will.

Most of us have preconceived notions, ideas or opinions based on what we have read or heard, perhaps by word of mouth, or from the television or other media such as newspapers; but if we have experienced a particular situation, then our awareness of the event may be considerably different from that of a possibly biased reporter. Political propaganda is a case in point. My husband was involved in such an incident.

While we were living in Accra, the capital of Ghana, West Africa, the Queen was due to visit. For weeks before her arrival, Gerald was heavily involved in the enormous preparations.

One Sunday morning he had a phone call from the local police station saying that a slightly crazy local—with absolutely no political affiliation, I might add—had set off a couple of homemade bombs, Molotov cocktails. These had caused some minor damage. The first chipped a couple of marble tiles at the base of the Triumphant Arch in Black Star Square; the other blew off one of the feet of President Kwama Nkrumah's statue.

The whole incident was more of a joke than anything to be taken seriously, particularly as Gerald got the local dentist to patch the president's foot with false-teeth plaster molding, then rub it with shoe polish, and finally, lacquer it so that no one could tell what was repaired.

That was the end of the incident as far as we were concerned, except to make amused comments about the local idol now having 'clay' feet!

A couple of days later, headlines appeared in world newspapers from Britain, the United States, Europe, Australia, Canada. All said roughly the same.

Bomb Outrage, Vast Damage to Accra, Political Unrest, Queen Must Not Go to Ghana, Her Life is in Danger

We had no idea to what the reporters were alluding until we scanned down to the details hidden in the political rhetoric.

It was appalling exaggeration based on this poor, local, crazy man's efforts. Apparently, one reporter had sent his version of the story to a news service from which major papers drew material. You can imagine the disturbance this caused, for at that time great efforts were being made to unify and consolidate peace efforts between African nations and the rest of the world: the very reason for the Queen's visit.

This is an example of misinterpretation of a situation leading to dangerous misconceptions. There had been no political connection; indeed, the plans for Her Majesty's visit were going along harmoniously. Calling it off could have caused considerable harm to those World Peace efforts, even disastrous repercussions.

I have to admit that I now rarely believe the exaggerations I read in the newspapers.

A more recent example of the power of the media was in the near-hysterical reaction to the tragic death of the Princess of Wales. There was, and rightly so, a deep and genuine regret for the destruction of a young and lovely person's life.

But it was followed by an unprecedented media-manufactured campaign in which the public was virtually blackmailed into condemnation of the whole Royal family. To me, one of the saddest parts of that whole tragic week was the scene of the Royals standing in lonely isolation at the gates of the palace watching the funeral cortege pass by.

There was an inference that only Diane mingled with the public; only Diane did good works; only Diane visited the sick and the suffering; only Diane supported worthy causes . . . and on and on and on.

This is not true.

Over the years, the Queen, Prince Philip, Prince Charles, Princess Anne, and others, each have quietly been involved in public service with the same efforts as were made so public by Diana. The lack of publicity of their activities has been deliberate, particularly as we now know what harm the paparazzi of the press can do. The daily lives of the Royals would be unendurable if they were constantly open to the eyes of the world.

But there are occasions when publicity is forced upon the Royal Family for political purposes, which brings me back to my original subject. The Queen's visit to Ghana.

For a full week after the bomb incident, editorials 'went to town' on political unrest on the African continent: interference in African affairs on the one hand, and danger to Her Majesty on the other.

Finally, the situation calmed (nothing so dead as yesterday's news), and reason prevailed; but, of course, there was no retraction from the world press. Nobody explained that the incidents were nothing more than a storm in a teacup.

So the Queen and Prince Philip arrived.

Until then, I had absolutely no idea what the poor woman had to endure.

They remained for ten days. At the end of it, I, who was lucky enough to be part of the tour—only part, with no duties other than to smile and look relaxed—was absolutely exhausted.

It was during her stay, I discovered just how much hard work the Queen had to do to insure the success of her visit, and how invaluable was her contribution to peace and international understanding.

I discovered that each night before she went to bed, she was given a long list of the people who would be introduced to her, and a piece of information about each person so that she could make interested, knowledgeable conversation. How flattered any of us would be if such consideration of us were given to make us feel important, be it by a queen or president.

I discovered that she never made a mistake and was equally charming to all.

I discovered that not only did she study her requirements for the following day, but she also, each night, read papers on the parliamentary proceedings back in Britain. Indeed, she is recognized as one of the most knowledgeable historians of European affairs.

I discovered that she had an intense desire to learn as much as she could about each event.

I discovered that she never allowed tiredness to show, that she was aware of how much her presence meant.

I discovered how genuinely she cared for people, how deeply concerned she was that every ounce of effort she was capable of giving was her duty to give.

I discovered that she was humbly dedicated to a life style that many times must have been almost unendurable. Imagine shaking hands with dozens and dozens of people day after day; of smiling, smiling, and never allowing irritation to show.

Let me describe just one day of her visit.

I was up at dawn, new dress, new hat, car brightly polished, chauffeur immaculate. Off we drove to join the royal procession. First stop Achimota School where a new wing was to be dedicated. Temperature somewhere in the nineties. All I had to do, with the rest of the party, was smile and follow the Queen and Prince Philip who each talked to all who were designated to be introduced.

I remember her first conversation: "I am delighted to meet you, Mr. Smith; I hear you have been doing remarkable research in the agriculture department." Of course, Mr. Smith was delighted to tell Her Majesty of his success.

The enormous crowds leaned forward to listen and reached to try to touch her at every opportunity. She showed no irritation, no impatience. By now, after more than a week, understanding the meaning of keeping one's cool, I was even more impressed by this remarkable woman.

Next stop, Legon University. Same format. Temperature even higher. I was already beginning to wilt with the pressure of the bodies, the noise, the dust. Yet Her Majesty showed no signs of the effect. I, who lived in that hot climate, wondered how much I could stand.

Next stop, the Y.M.C.A., and then the blind school, and then the market. I did not attend that last visit. The flies and the smell were always indescribable. But the Queen stoically ploughed on, going from stall to stall and speaking to those who worked there, though they were not on any list of important people.

And those were just the morning's events.

At noon, Her Majesty and Prince Philip were whisked back to Christiansburg Castle for a quick change of clothes, then to a private luncheon with those most closely involved with her visit.

After the lunch, she gave a private audience to each individual, including my husband, again knowing what each person had done, and personally thanking them.

Next came the races. A nice bit of relaxation? Hardly, since the people were far more interested in the Royals than the horses!

After the races, another quick change into ball clothes and jewels and on to a diplomatic reception where she made a speech. This was followed by a state dinner . . . and yet another speech.

Then to the State Ball held in the enormous plaza in front of the State House. Over a thousand people attended. It was almost a disaster as there were many with illegal tickets, which some bright entrepreneur had copied. Yet the Queen danced and smiled, and danced and smiled.

At midnight, I was standing beside her in the foyer as she was about to leave. An extremely drunken Ghanaian lady stumbled her way to the front and removed a voluminous gold cloak she was wearing and spread it in front of Her Majesty.

"Sir Walter Raleigh laid down his cloak for the other Queen Elizabeth, please step on mine."

We all froze in horror.

How would the Queen handle what could be an indelicate situation?

She merely carried on the conversation she was having with others around her, ignoring the action as if she had not heard. No embarrassment, no turning away, no sign of displeasure. Eventually, the woman uncertainly picked up her cloak and staggered off mumbling to herself.

Of course, I was filled with an enormous admiration for the Queen's aplomb, but for one poignant moment I was also filled with an enormous sympathy, for as she turned her head to the people around her, I noticed that, under her beautiful tiara, in the hot and humid atmosphere, her hair was just as untidy as mine certainly was. And that was the only external effect she showed after fifteen grueling hours.

But there were humorous moments over which I'm sure Philip and she must have chuckled; incidents which, perhaps, lightened and made endurable that fish-bowl-like existence.

I mentioned how various people, including my husband, were given a private audience so that the Queen could thank them for all their efforts. Over those last few pressure-filled weeks of preparation for the visit, one of his responsibilities was the improvement necessary to Christiansburg Castle where the Queen and Prince Philip were to stay.

New bathrooms had been constructed on the top floor where the royal apartments were to be. The water was piped there on a gravity feed system. On the morning the royal party were due to arrive, Gerald checked the castle, and even turned on all the taps in the royal suite to make sure everything was functioning perfectly.

At seven in the evening, the party arrived. At 7:30 Gerald received a frantic phone call from one of the ladies-in-waiting.

"There is no water in Her Majesty's bathroom!"

Gerald was horrified. That had been the last room he had checked. There had been plenty of water then. Abjectly, he apologized, wanting to go over to the castle immediately to find out the cause. On being told that tomorrow would do, and that the Queen would use another bathroom for now, Gerald racked his brains to try to work out what had gone wrong.

As soon as her Majesty left in the morning to go to her various functions, he hurried into her bathroom and turned on the taps.

Plenty of water!

Then he realized what had happened.

When, after her arrival at the castle, the Queen had retired to freshen up before dinner, so had everyone else. All had turned on taps at approximately the same time, and the water was drawn off at the lowest points first; hence, none had reached the bathroom of her royal personage!

Full of abject apologies for not having realized that this would happen, Gerald promised to fix the problem, which he duly did by having a new tank installed. But the damage had been done. In all the thousand and one responsibilities he took care of during the royal visit, why did the one thing that went wrong have to be so personal to Her Majesty?

Gerald had a burning desire to apologize for this mistake, which had been intensely embarrassing. This private meeting after the luncheon was his opportunity. He hardly ate anything, worrying over just how he could explain why the problem had happened.

After being greeted by the Queen at the private audience, and listening to her kind words of thanks for all his efforts, at last Gerald began to make his apologies.

"Ma'am," he stuttered, so concerned that she should understand the reason for the empty taps, "I do apologize for the trouble you had with your water."

For a moment, stunned silence. Appalled at what he had said, but not knowing how to extract his foot from his mouth, he waited for some sort of scathing comment, particularly as Prince Philip had a decidedly thunderous expression on his face.

"*Mr. Nugent*," said her Majesty, with a wide grin and a chuckle; "*I assure you, there was no problem with my water.*"

She knew exactly to what he was alluding, understood the embarrassment of his gaff, and wanted to save him further apologies. She shook his hand, thanked him again for all his efforts, and with great relief, he staggered out of the room.

How could one not love a woman who so kindly and graciously understood and forgave what was probably the most embarrassing moment of my husband's life?

So you see, Her Majesty is not just an expensive figurehead, she is a hard-working, caring person who has given a lifetime of duty, not only to Britain but also to the world.

And since at the beginning of this chapter I mentioned 'expensive', the world needs clarification on how much of her own money she quietly uses.

Did you know that the Queen paid for the royal wedding of Charles and Diana in its entirety, except for the police? Did you also know that it engendered over a billion dollars in television moneys and in tourist revenues, none of which she accepted?

And her overseas visits. These do bring advancement to those countries in so many ways. Public services are improved; tourism developed, and deeper, world-wide understanding of their people, which increases national prestige. Gerald was involved in much of that in Ghana. The harbor, roads, buildings all benefited. We perhaps can understand this through the similar impact of the Olympic Games. A royal visit can be even more beneficial.

I am so grateful that I was in Ghana when the Queen came to visit. I became aware of the immense value of the Royal Family, and will never again think of it as an out-of-date anachronism in our fast-paced world. Indeed, the crown has a stature above even its present wearer.

On June the 15th, 1215, the barons at Runnymede protested in the Magna Carter that the royal crown in the hands of King John was being abused, was out of date. And protests have been made regularly down the centuries, even to the beheading of one king.

Yet nearly eight hundred years later, we still are proud of our royal heritage and have deep admiration for the crown's present wearer who has shown great willingness to move into the twenty-first century. She now pays income tax; receives less money from the government for the upkeep of her position than does the President of the United States; pays for other Royals, who still do their same public duty; pays personally for much of the maintenance of royal property, and is putting on display far more of the crown's treasures than before, though many of them are her own personal property. And monies collected do not go into her pocket but to public charities.

I am sure that there have been many days when she wished she could run away from it all and live a private life like the rest of us. I know I could never begin to endure the ugly spotlight of the media as she so heroically has always done.

But among all the pomp and ceremony of that royal visit, there was one tiny incident, which touched me personally.

I was standing by the royal dais at the official garden party waiting for Prince Philip to pass my way, hoping he would stop. He chatted to the ladies since the Queen's duty was to speak to the men. She had already returned and was standing waiting for her husband to finish.

Suddenly, I was aware of someone looking at me.

I turned.

It was Her Majesty.

She had a delightful grin on her face. She raised her hand to the hat on her head and nodded at mine. I was wearing a glorious, huge, white-fringed, cartwheel, garden party concoction.

I just knew she was implying, "I like your hat."

But there was another less-than-euphoric occasion when my name was almost mud.

Weeks before the State Ball, Gerald, in his position of authority, arranged that we should have a table for twelve at that function.

"You can invite five other couples," he said; "but select then with care. They have to be appropriate for the occasion." That meant I couldn't just ask my tennis buddies.

Oh dear. I went through my list of fuddy-duddies: The Minister of this, the Chief Secretary of that . . . and their often snooty wives.

Before I actually sent out the invitations, it was surprising how many friends I had! Or was it?

76

The evening arrived. We were all to meet for cocktails at our house at 5:30 p.m., giving us an hour before we had to leave in time to reach the State House gates. They were to close at 7:30 and there was sure to be a long queue. Gerald promised to arrive from work as soon as he could, and we were to have drinks and hors d'oeuvres while we waited for him. I had his evening clothes all ready. Surely he wouldn't be late. Worriedly we watched the clock. 6:30 arrived, then 7:00, then 7:30. Oh, was my name mud?

Far from polite complaints. My guests were now openly agreeing that they should have known better than to accept my invitation.

I was desolate, profuse in apologies, but there was nothing I could do.

Then Gerald appeared, all smiles. "I'll only be five minutes."

He rushed through the briefest of showers, then bustled us out to the cars. I kept silent, trying to smile. Our guests were grim faced. This was the occasion of the century and they would miss it. After all, the gates would be locked long before we got to the State House.

Not surprisingly, the roads were empty, for every other invitee had arrived long ago.

We reached the gates, which as I expected were closed. Gerald was still smiling.

The soldier on duty, as soon as he saw big Massa, opened them and waved us through. I breathed a sigh of relief. But the vast car-parking area was totally full. Now what?

Still smiling, Gerald drove up the long driveway to the State House.

I was holding my breath.

There, in front of the huge portal, were a group of soldiers guarding some empty parking places.

The sergeant saluted and signaled for three of these spaces to be opened . . . and Gerald, unconcerned, parked our car. Our guests, no doubt in shock, parked behind.

Of course, the other spaces were for the entourage of Kwami Nkrumah and the Queen!

By now, it was almost eight, and the Royals would soon be arriving.

We hurriedly followed Gerald as he marched through the imposing entrance.

We reached the plaza where the ball was being held. It was full. More than full. Not a seat in sight, much less a table.

My hopes that had been rising plummeted once again.

Still Gerald was unconcerned.

Another group of soldiers was guarding an area just inside the entrance.

They were galvanized into action when they saw my husband.

A small door at the side was opened. Four burly men brought out a table and placed it in the space where they had been standing. More brought out chairs. Others produced table linen, cutlery, china and glasses, then conducted us to our seats.

All wonderful, and such a relief. But better and better. Our table was next to the dais where The Royal Group were to sit.

Within minutes, they arrived to take their places . . .

Apart from theirs, we had the best seats in the house. But I could have shot my complacent husband who had enjoyed every minute of my near despair.

Of course, we didn't dance very much; we mostly sat google eyed watching Her Majesty. Such a lovely, lovely evening.

And afterward, we had what was probably the best time of the night.

When the Royal party and all the invitees left, Gerald and various of our male guests had to stay behind for a conference. I and some of the wives stayed, too.

A waiter brought us champagne and fresh glasses, and we seated ourselves on the Royal thrones. There was nobody to complain, for after all, my husband was the boss.

When our glasses were empty, the same waiter brought us more. I noticed it was a fresh bottle, but surely there had been some champagne left in the first bottle?

Some three, or four, maybe more bottles later, I don't know who was more tipsy, we, or the waiter; for I had a good guess who had drunk the last of that champagne in each bottle.

Only later did I discover that it was the Queen's private supply.

WORDS, WORDS, WORDS

Soon after this, we finally retired and returned to England. We were sad to leave, for we had loved the life, but independent Ghana was determined to rule itself and no longer felt it needed British help.

We bought a house and I settled down to being a typical house-wife. Oh my! That was coming down to earth. No more helpful servants.

I produced another child, and my life became one of changing diapers and scrubbing the kitchen floor.

Not that I minded really; Greg and Rachel made new friends and baby Giles was an amusing bundle. Like any mother, if one's children are happy, then all's right with the world.

But Gerald found his new job so narrow after the huge responsibilities he had held in Ghana, and after a few years, he began to look around for pastures new.

Casual conversation with a visiting Canadian resulted in an offer of a contract to help build a Kraft mill, the headquarters to be in Montreal. The pay was twice his present salary . . . and what could be so difficult about building a cheese factory?

The documents were signed and sealed and we prepared to pack up, all excited about our new adventure. Then Gerald got his first shock. When talking to a neighbor, he discovered that a Kraft mill had nothing to do with cheese. Kraft meant paper. He had signed a contract to help build a paper mill . . . about which, he knew nothing.

Ah well. 'Nothing' phased my supremely confident husband, this extremely competent engineer. What's in a name, anyway? This neighbor arranged for Gerald to visit a local paper mill. His education on its construction amounted to that one day only. Hardly the proverbial 'piece of cake'!

I remember when he returned from that visit, he was rather silent.

But the contract had been signed; Gerald had plenty of qualifications and experience in all kinds of engineering, and he always loved a challenge.

Within weeks, on New Year's Eve, we were on the plane having sold the house and most of the contents. I had been far too busy to worry about what was going to happen when we arrived in Canada.

Nobody met us, but we were booked into the Holiday Inn so went there and waited. Two days later, still nobody had called, so Gerald decided he had better go to his new office and present himself.

Can you imagine him walking into reception and saying, "I'm Gerald Nugent," and getting a non-plus reaction of, "So?"

In retrospect, it was funny, but not at the time. He was taken in to see the managing director who was equally puzzled.

"You say you have a contract?" Gerald had had the presence of mind to take it with him. He pointed out the signature of the man who had signed it.

Dawning understanding. Then, "No wonder I know nothing about you. That man left the company three weeks ago."

Gerald said afterward that the vision of him with a wife and three children standing in the bitter cold of a Canadian winter, with no home, no job, no prospects, was the worst moment of his life.

But I still grin at what happened next.

"Well, you have a contract. We will, of course, honor it. Go and get your family settled and come back in three days. Between now and then, I'll decide how we shall use you."

And so we did. We rented an apartment, bought a car and moved out of the hotel.

So far, so good.

When Gerald returned to the office, the manager had made a decision.

"Since you are an expert in Kraft paper mills . . ." (Imagine even 'I-can-do-anything-Gerald' startled at the implication.) "I'm sending you to Newfoundland where we desperately need a new railroad system round the complex."

In some relief, Gerald accepted his orders. This, he could do.

He was there for a week working on the plans, which proved to be more difficult than he expected, for though the mill covered a huge area it was on a narrow spit of land. He returned to head office, rather proud of his efforts.

He laid out his detailed design for the manager to approve.

Curious, rather bewildered reaction.

"Er. What is this?" He pointed to various double lines going round the buildings.

"That's the road." Surely he could understand that.

"But why? I didn't ask for a road."

"Yes you did," (My husband has been known to be belligerent when he knows he is right.) "You asked for a rail-road system."

Dawning, rather amused understanding. "Of course, I should have explained knowing you were just out of England. A railroad system in this country means a rail line, one rail line, not a line including a road."

But it all turned out well. It had not been thought possible to fit in a new road, so Gerald came out smelling like a rose. Of course, now he was considered a real expert on Kraft Paper mills . . . though we were learning fast that our two countries don't speak the same language.

There was another occasion where I learned of another word with a different meaning . . .

We had been in Montreal about three weeks and a kindly neighbor invited us to a cocktail party. I knew nobody there and was a little uncertain just how to behave in this new country. For once, I was keeping quiet, speaking only when spoken to.

Somebody took pity on me and politely tried to start a conversation.

"And tell me, Mrs. Nugent, why have you and your husband decided to come to our country?"

Honesty is always the best policy, Yes?

"Quite frankly, because my husband has a better screw over here."

A moment's silence. Then great guffaws of laughter.

I had no idea why what I had said was so funny. I was not ashamed to admit that a better salary had persuaded us to come. Oh dear. I blushingly sidled over to Gerald and asked him why everyone had laughed.

Drat the man. He laughed, too.

"I'll tell you later," was all he would say. It was just as well he didn't tell me then. I'd have died of embarrassment. After all, everyone in England knew that a screw was a salary; surely the Canadians did, too. So what was so funny?

But that's not the end of the story.

Three weeks later, Gerald was talking to a business connection in Vancouver way across the other side of the continent.

When they had finished, the man said, "I've a funny story I know you'll appreciate. Did you hear the one about the English girl who came over to Canada and went to a cocktail party . . . ?

Just three weeks it had taken for that story to travel four thousand miles . . . It's no wonder I decided to called this chapter . . .
WORDS, WORDS, WORDS.

CATS

A couple of years later, we moved to Niagara Falls. Our family had now increased with the birth of another little girl.

Gerald came home from work one Monday morning only having been there for an hour.

"Would you like to go to Dhaka?" he asked.

"Sure." I replied. Quite often I would go with him if he had a day's business trip. The older children were at school, and baby Rowena loved the car.

"Where's Dhaka?"

"Pakistan."

"Pakistan?" I gulped. All sorts of questions tumbled out, but finally the most important. "When?"

"Friday."

Now my husband has thrown me some curved balls in his time, and usually I have managed to cope. Once, we had moved into a new house and were transferred two days later, but I didn't have four children then.

Friday . . . only three full days. Impossible. Well, almost.

I began to pack. I arranged for stuff to go into storage, luggage to go by sea, cases for our traveling. I rented the house, sold the car, and made appointments for inoculations and vaccinations for all of us. I seemed to spend hours on the phone tying up enormous amounts of arrangements. Thank heavens the children were excited by the move.

In amongst all this, we shopped. We were going to a much hotter part of the world than Niagara Falls, Canada, and all of us needed completely new wardrobes and, of course, plenty of books, educational and otherwise, and loads of drug store items ranging from aspirins to calamine lotion. We bought new, matching suitcases, for we had so much to pack,

Gerald was working early and late trying to make all the preparations needed for this new engineering project, so he was able to give very little help; yet somehow, we managed.

We broke our journey for a few days in England, then on to Turkey where we looked forward to introducing the children to a more exotic European country. We left all our luggage at the airport except one suitcase containing clothes and toiletries for the three days we would be staying in Istanbul. I had packed it very carefully.

We took a taxi to the Hilton to book rooms . . . only to find there were none available: some sort of World Conference was going on. All other hotels the receptionist called for us were also booked solid.

We tried the various embassies with no success. By now I was getting desperate. It was evening, and I was having visions of us all sleeping on park benches.

Then I remembered an old Turkish friend from more than twenty years ago. He had been my partner on my college tennis team. When I located him in the telephone book and called him, he found us a couple of rooms in a friend's apartment. Relieved, exhausted, and extremely grateful, we began to settle for the night. I opened the suitcase to take out pajamas and found . . . we had brought the wrong one. So much for the elegance of matching luggage. School books stared up at me as I lifted the lid.

Ah well. We'd all just have to sleep in our underwear.

At last, we were settled.

Then began a drama that stretched our parenting capabilities to the limit. I woke to hear two sounds. One, that of cats mewing at the door, and the other, Greg wheezing dreadfully He was extremely allergic to furry animals. Dear heavens! What could we do? His medication was in the luggage at the airport; without it, he could go into a coma?

We had no choice, we had to leave.

Dragging the protesting children out of bed, we dressed them, and leaving some money on the table, crept out of the apartment into the dawn. We had no idea what we were going to do as we walked down the hill. No one was out at that early hour; but perhaps we could find an all-night cafe; anywhere that we could sit and have breakfast. At least, Greg's wheezing was beginning to ease in the fresh morning air, even though he was still staggering in a daze. Perhaps we wouldn't need to take him to hospital . . . if we could find one. Even Gerald's usual cool was badly shaken.

A taxi, the only vehicle we had seen so far, drew up beside us, and a most concerned driver, in rather broken English, asked if we needed help. I think he was so startled to see such a raggle-taggle of crying children, and obviously distraught parents. Asking no more questions, he bundled us into his cab with promises to solve all our problems.

And solve then, he did. He found us a small hotel—much beneath the dignity of the Hilton, but we didn't care.

He was so kind. He left us there, promising to come back later, after the children had slept, and take us on a tour of the city.

Then followed the most wonderful three days. The dear man took us everywhere; the Blue Mosque, Topkapi Museum, Atta Turk's extraordinary palace, St. David's Towers. He drove us beside the Bosphorus to the Black Sea, found delicious restaurants where the children gorged themselves on shrimp and lobster. He even drove us through the Golden Horn to the vast, covered market of a thousand shops where we were able to replenish our non-existent wardrobe.

Greg, particularly, had a ball. His allergies quickly dried up, and he was fascinated by the strange places and objects. Even to this day, he has a great curiosity about the world around us, and a prodigious memory.

In the museum, there was a large elephant about two feet tall. The guide told him he could have it if he could pick it up. We tried not to laugh as he struggled, quite determined to take it away. Of course, he couldn't even shift it, for it was solid gold and must have weighed hundreds of pounds.

As the day passed, one or other child would fall asleep, and our kind driver would babysit. I look back now and wonder how we dared trust this unknown man while the rest of us visited particular sites. But trust him, we did. And when he dropped us at the airport three days later, he would only accept twenty dollars in payment. I wondered if that even covered the gasoline.

But it was the best twenty dollars we have ever spent, and we will never forget our angel of mercy. Or the cats!

HANDSOME HARRY

From Istanbul we flew to East Pakistan, to Gerald's new project. As we landed, we were all excited to see this new land. But my first introduction as we left the plane was not what I expected.

I had traveled enough not usually to be shocked, but Handsome Harry, a well know local character, was an ugly site. With a wide grin on his face, he held out his begging bowl for 'buckshee' (alms).

Handsome Harry had no nose.

I remember how I flinched.

He smiled at us, pointing quite cheerfully to the gap.

In some horror, I muttered to Gerald that surely with modern medical science, a new nose could be built. My cynical husband then told me a few harsh facts of life . . . intermingled with lessons in generosity.

There are many beggars in Pakistan, and most countries in the East, and Harry, just one of them, had made himself worthy of that title, particularly as these kindly people will always give something to help these sad cases.

But Gerald's cynicism didn't stop there.

"He's on to a good thing. He probably is quite a wealthy man by local standards. He certainly doesn't want his nose repaired. He'd have to find a job!"

I struggled to find a moral in there somewhere but decided that I must not judge such a different way of life, much as I deplored it.

On another occasion, I met a similar deformity.

We were in the market one Saturday afternoon looking for a birthday present for the children to take to a party. It was a hot day and the rancid smell of cooking, the cacophony of bleating goats and squawking chickens, and the general hubbub of arguing merchants was giving my quite a headache. I went to stand in the shade.

I was suddenly conscious of something touching my leg. I looked down at the bright-eyed smile of a small child squatting on the ground. He couldn't have been more than two.

He pointed to his shoulder. Perched over it was his foot. Yes, his foot. I shuddered at what I saw. His leg was twisted and deformed.

In horror, I ran to the car where I waited, shivering, for my family to return.

This time, I learned two lessons.

The first one was similar to that of Handsome Harry . . . a proudly displayed begging tool was an assurance that its owner would never starve. In order for a family with too many children to be sure that each would survive, it was not uncommon for limbs to be broken and bent at birth so that the child would always be able to beg. Five hundred years ago in Europe, this same method of survival was used. Terrible, ugly, ghastly in this day and age, but criticism was not my right.

The second lesson I learned is one I still call my hair shirt. Ascetics years ago punished themselves by wearing a rough, scratchy garment so they would remember their sins. I have never forgotten mine, which was the sin of running away.

I discovered I was not a good Samaritan, for behaving as the Levy, I did nothing to help.

Of course, there was nothing I could do, short of giving alms, but that's not the point.

The point was that I didn't even try. I ran away, seeing only the horror, not seeing the innocence of the child.

THE CHRISTMAS PRESENT

Life is such a mixture of the poignant sadness and the hilariously absurd, as we learned one particular Christmas Day.

Gerald had had to return to Canada for a week on emergency business, leaving us behind in East Pakistan. I, somewhat disgruntled, lonely and miserable, dutifully tried to make the day cheerful and festive for the children. None of us really felt in the Christmas spirit; but knowing this was what Daddy wanted, we bundled into the car and were driven to Dhaka Cathedral to celebrate the Holy Day.

The temperature was in the eighties and we were hot and sticky. The usual plethora of flies buzzed around, no doubt enjoying our discomfort. The children were glum. I was glum. It just didn't seem like Christmas without Daddy. I had my sun glasses on hoping no one would see the tears I was trying to control.

The service droned on. I was much too full of my misery and the unfairness of life—head office in particular—to pay much attention.

Suddenly, there was a faint murmur in the church, a restlessness. My head had been bowed, but now I looked up. The murmur grew and changed into laughter. I turned my head wondering what was so amusing.

At the side of the long nave was a high pulpit rarely used since the priest mostly stood at the altar. There were steps up to this lectern and a chair placed conveniently for him if he needed to rest after preaching from there. My eyes followed those of the congregation who by now were pointing in that direction and beginning to laugh. Above the noise I heard a happy voice.

"Hi, Mom."

It was that of my two-year-old daughter Rowena.

She had become bored, and Mummy was paying no attention, so she had got to her little feet and wandered from the pew to a higher place. When she reached the top of the pulpit steps, she climbed onto the chair and leaned over to survey the assembled company.

Big beaming smile, quite happy to be the center of attention, and much more able to see what was going on, she rested her chin on her little hands, deciding that this was the place to be.

My other three naughty children thought this was great fun and laughed as loudly as the rest of the congregation. Only when they saw my consternation did Greg fetch her down.

87

But she had made our day. We chuckled all the way home with less than reverend jokes about the arrival of the Christ Child. Christmas became again a day of joy and gratitude. My four wonderful children and I had so much to be thankful for, particularly the special gift of laughter.

THE BALUCHISTANI WOMEN

Golf was very much part of our life when we were in East Pakistan, and during the winter months we played almost every evening. Beautiful weather, blue skies, temperatures usually in the seventies and low eighties. Gerald and I even won the local championship and were invited to play in one in West Pakistan, the other side of India.

Looking back, it's amusing to remember how we thought nothing of traveling great distances for an event in Africa. We'd drive 350 miles to a weekend party. This journey was more, though, almost 1,500 miles, but just a few hours by plane.

We landed in Rawalpinda and were driven from there to the Abbottabad golf course, and to our accommodation for the two-day tournament. (Incidentally, Abbottabad is the military town where Bin Laden lived for years before he was found and killed by the Americans.)

We stayed in the Circuit Judge's rest house. Quite an honor, we were told, though we would have liked some air-conditioning, for the days were hotter than we had expected.

The houseman produced for us, with great pride, the sheets we were to have on our beds. He unfolded them pointing out the exquisite embroidery on each. Mine was covered with roses, and Gerald had peacocks all over his. We looked suitably impressed.

And that was just what we were when we woke up in the morning. The embroidery, beautiful though it was, had been done in rather thick thread, so each of us was imprinted with the patterns. My husband looked rather cute with peacocks fluttering up his back.

The golf was fun. We didn't win, of course, but we met many delightful people; Gerald even won a trophy for something or other. When it was over, we decided to take advantage of the extra day of our long weekend break and explore.

Being quite near to Kashmir, we were loaned a car and a driver and were driven up to Murree in the foothills of the Himalayas. We weren't able to go over the border because the interminable fracas between India and Pakistan was ongoing: too many guns popping off. But we enjoyed what turned out to be quite a tourist town.

We meandered through the local market admiring the fruit and nuts on display. Peaches, apricots, melons, almonds, walnuts; as good as any I had seen in other parts of the world.

I also saw more of the same embroidery we had 'made contact with' in the rest house, and different, delicate handwork on the finest of muslim. I bought a set of table mats far too thin for practical use, but I couldn't resist them. I had bought linen tablecloths in the Canary Islands, and hand woven ones in Ghana, but none quite so exquisite as these.

As we wandered, I saw a group of women seated at the side of the road. They were dressed in vivid, gypsy-like clothes. I stared in fascination. Their full, red-brown skirts, cinched tightly at narrow waists, reached down to high, leather riding boots. Their blouses were of this same fine muslim as my new table mats, embroidery over every part including the wide sleeves.

Around each forehead was a band of coins that jangled and sparkled in the sunlight. On their heads were veils edged with more of this same embroidery. Black, black hair in loose, curling strands hung forward over their shoulders.

They had extraordinarily beautiful faces, pale-skinned, Caucasian featured, with the slender aquiline noses inherited, no doubt, from distant Greek ancestry. Around 300 B.C. Alexander the Great had invaded South East Asia, hoping to loot the fabulous wealth of India. Many of his soldiers had settled, intermarried, producing a race of tall, strong North West Frontier men who reminded me of ancient Olympians, much different from the smaller, slenderer East Pakistanis.

These women had the same statuesque physique

Their green-brown eyes had the curious creamy flecked irises, common to so many of these people: bright and vivid: none of the more faded blues or grays we see in our Northern climes, nor the darker brown of southern European or African heritage.

Our driver told me that these women were Baluchistanis from southern Pakistan and had come for some sort of festival.

I moved closer, spell bound.

Realizing what a marvelous opportunity I had to photograph such a charming scene, I took out my camera and smiled hopefully at them so they would perhaps smile and pose for me.

What a shock I got.

One of the women jumped to her feet, rage clearly showing on her face. She charged toward me, raised whip in her hand. Then she began to beat me.

I turned and ran, quite shattered at the anger I had unleashed, not understanding why.

Yet my overall impression was of majesty. This woman dominated me as queenlike as any I had ever seen. I was in awe at her sheer magnificence.

Gerald was all concerned as I, no doubt as white as a sheet, hurried toward him. At first he was worried at the marks on my face until I explained what had happened. Then he began to laugh.

"No wonder she was furious. I should have told you. You don't know how fearful these people are of having their photographs taken. They think it will take away not only their souls, but also their ability to have children."

Yet another lesson learned. In this modern world, perhaps it is sad that such ignorance should still exist. But my admiration didn't lessen as I watched them climb onto their horses and ride away as free as the wind.

I found much to admire in these people and felt quite humble when I learned just how old was their civilization. When we returned to Rawalpinda to catch our plane back to Dhaka, we bought some cutlery that had the motive of a very virile bull. It was a copy of engravings on the wall of Mohenjo-daro, a city over 5,000 years old, which sadly lies in ruins, though much preservation work has been done. This city in the Indus valley far to the south, near to Baluchistan, had a remarkably advanced society and is reputed to have the earliest example of public hot baths. Curious to think that they were developing their culture at the same time as the Egyptians: millenniums before the English had stopped dancing around in their painted blue woad.

DIFFERENCES

Each country and culture has variations from which we can learn. Unfortunately, we tend to assume that we know better and are not very good at keeping an open mind. We are not prepared to understand the reasoning behind our differences. The Hindus don't eat beef, the Moslems, pork. Even the Japanese won't eat blue cheese. But we have no right to criticize

My mother once said to me, "If I have an opinion, a really strong opinion, it is that, I don't have an opinion."

It has taken me many years of travel to really understand what she meant. Basically, she deplored bigoted intolerance, and the complacency that comes from, 'What's good enough for my father is good enough for me.' She never condemned or criticized; always tried to understand. "Criticism of others comes from complacency and ignorance within ourselves," was a lesson she taught me.

Easily enough said, but sometimes such lessons are hard to learn, though I now, frankly, think complacency is the eighth deadly sin . . . as in the following story.

One day in Pakistan, the cook came to me and said, "Small boy sick. No can wash kitchen floor."

Now I was adamant that this had to be done every day.

"Then get the garden boy to do it." I said.

I was told he wouldn't. It was not his job.

I went through the list of servants, but no one was prepared to scrub.

Of course, I who had high principles of all work being honorable, decided to teach them a lesson. Naturally, I was right. I knew better than this bunch of lazy servants.

I decided to show them an example, that, in my opinion, there was nothing undignified in getting down on one's hands and knees and scrubbing a kitchen floor, which I proceeded to do.

Oh dear. I was the one who learned a lesson.

All of the servants walked out.

This was when I discovered one of the differences in our cultures.

They had walked out because they would not work for someone who was lower than they were in their scale of authority. And I had just placed myself at the bottom of that scale.

Now the nearest I suppose I can equate their reasoning is to what our western men adhere to years ago. "I don't do that. It's woman's work." Though, thankfully, things have changed in Europe and America, I had no right to contradict what was based on their years of tradition.

So much for inflicting my opinion.

What was worse, none of the servants came back, and I had considerable difficulty in finding any more. The word had gone out.

"That Madam, she scrub kitchen floor."

But there is a cultural reason for this eastern attitude and this traditional adherence to hierarchy, which has applied to people in this part of the world.

Until more recent years, the oldest member had been the decision maker. Until that member died, whoever was next in line, however old, would not contradict or usurp his authority. Consequently, new ideas have been slow to filter. But much as we may feel this is antediluvian, it has been a way to prevent the discarding of the older people. It has its value, for we, in our culture, have lost this loving care and respect for the aged.

So we are not always right in our opinions. And this was another eye-opening example when I learned that others are not always wrong!

Of course, I found the humorous side to many of our differences. We try to inflict our language and meanings, particularly in religion, on other races. Sometimes, the garbled versions are quite delightful.

A missionary was trying to translate the Bible into an African tribe's local dialect. Since they had no conception of what the poor man was trying to tell them, they created their own picture in their own language.

"This God man? Who be he?"

The missionary explained as best he could and quoted, 'Our Father who art in heaven.'

Dawning understanding.

"Ahhh . . . Big Massa dey for topside. Yes?"

It's good not to be too sanctimonious about actual words. The African is so descriptive and his word pictures, so graphic. A helicopter is 'big bird, fan dey for topside'. When the sea is calm, our steward once said, "Sea, he go sleep."

But my favorite story about other nations' misunderstanding of our language concerns our house boy Christian when we lived in Dunkwa.

Christian had been working for us for a year and wanted to go to the big city to find a better job. He was a good worker, and we happily encouraged him. Armed with letters of recommendation, he set off for Accra.

We heard nothing for a couple of weeks; then we got a phone call from a possible future employer.

He asked us the usual sorts of questions about Christian, and we assured him that all we had put in our letters was true.

"Is there a problem?" we asked.

"Well, there is just one thing . . ." The man seemed to be amused about something. "He's filled in the section that asks for next of kin."

"But he's an orphan," we replied.

"Not according to this application."

"Who's he put down?" we queried.

"He's written, Mrs. Nugent."

How sweet, I thought. "I don't mind." After all, I had been a sort of surrogate parent to him. "I don't have a problem with that."

He chuckled. "It's the relationship that's a problem."

"Relationship?" I didn't understand.

"Yes. He's written '*Mistress*'." The man couldn't restrain his laughter. "I hardly think your husband would approve. What would you like me to change that to?"

Now this was quite delicious. I had never in my life reached the status of mistress. Much too carefully brought up and prudish.

"No. Leave it." I loved it.

Language is a beautiful thing, don't you think?

NEPAL

I've not always been on the good end of a bargain, but I was once; though typical of human nature, I wish I had taken greater advantage of the opportunity.

Gerald was to examine the possibility of extending the Nepalese airport and needed to visit the site. The country was just beginning to open up to the tourist trade.

Of course, I wanted to go, too. I would have loved to have taken the children with us, but we were uncertain of conditions, both political- and comfort-wise, so we left them with friends.

We flew north from Dhaka to Katmandu, the capital, in a small plane with room for perhaps twenty. I remember how it rattled, but no one aboard seemed concerned.

Perhaps we'll see Everest, I hoped, so we climbed up through the foothills to the mountains beyond, but the cloud accumulation of the beginning of the monsoon season lay like a blanket over most of them. Only the peaks were visible, and the whole scene looked much like the top of one of my mother's Christmas cake where her fork had spiked the icing. Since eleven of the tallest mountains in the world are in the Himalayas, and the rest of this 2,000 mile range has others almost as high, I could only guess which was Everest. A passenger did point it out, but I have to confess I was little the wiser.

As we began to descend through a mountain pass, this same passenger told me a wonderful story concerning the birth of Katmandu. Now it was probably mostly myth, but later, when we went to play golf on the King of Nepal's private course, the very terrain suggested it might be true.

A thousand years ago, the then king wanted more land for his people. His palace was at the side of a lake, which filled most of the valley. Collecting all the able-bodies men, he took them to the lowest edge of the valley between two mountains and had them dig and dig until the restraining wall of rock broke away allowing the waters of the lake to drain out.

I suspect the cleft between the mountains was created by normal geological settling, but there certainly had been a lake there at some time since the hillocks and dips of the King's course meander just like mud flats after a storm. The tee to a hole could be fifty feet above a winding chasm, down which we would have to go before climbing up to the other side where would be the 'green.'

95

Nothing like any other greens I had seen. They were oiled earth, and even the merest tap sent one's golf ball slithering off the other side. Sometimes, on the longer holes, there were small arrowed signs by each tee indicating the direction of the green . . . and the distance. We might have to go up and down a couple more chasms before we reached that hole. We spent a delightful afternoon there, but our golf score was abysmal. Six-putting those greens didn't help.

Most of the rest of those three days, Gerald was meeting with officials, and I wandered up and down the streets, thoroughly enjoying myself.

The Nepalese are such a friendly people. They always seem to be smiling, and their apple cheeks are creased with laugh lines. Something about the air, I was told. Living at eight thousand feet in that clean, rarified atmosphere, with no enemies to worry them, seems to have developed a happy outlook on life that I wished I could bottle and take away with me.

But I did take away something.

I was wandering down a street of shops when I came to one that had huge peach baskets filled to overflowing. Not with peaches, but with semi-precious jewels.

I went inside.

The smiling, brown-skinned little man waved a hand asking me to help myself.

I became fascinated.

I delved into a basket and took out a handful of sparkling gems, then another handful. Spreading them on the counter, I began to separate them into little piles. I had no idea what they cost, but perhaps I could buy one or two . . . or three.

There were some particularly beautiful black star sapphires. By now I was like a small child playing with pebbles at the seaside. I searched through more of the gems until I had collected two matching sets of four graduating sapphires; I could visualize drop ear rings: beautiful, gold, drop ear rings.

Of course, like Aladdin in his cave, I didn't know when to stop. I collected lapis lazuli, aquamarines, topaz, a huge black onyx, even a couple of rings with set-in stones, one with a ruby, another with three matching pearls.

Oh, I had a wonderful time. Then I came down to earth. My dear, sweet husband spoiled me quite rotten, but even he was going to balk at the hefty price.

I piled all the stones into the palms of my hands and asked, "How much?" May be I could afford just one or two.

96

"Twenty dollars." said the shop keeper.

"For each?" I asked.

"For all," he answered in some surprise.

Now fool that I was, I was so stunned that I meekly handed over the bill.

What I should have remembered was that in Asian markets one only expects to pay half of the asking price. I could have got them for ten dollars. And what was even more stupid of me, I could have got another handful for the same price.

But isn't that human nature? If he had said forty dollars and I had bargained him down to half the price, I would have been thrilled with my purchase.

Years later, when Gerald went back by himself to Katmandu and tried to buy some more stones, the price had increased astronomically; the tourists had discovered this mine of goodies.

So now I am a little less mercenary and much more appreciative of my lovely jewelry . . . and Gerald is secretly glad that he could buy no more, for the cost of having my handfuls set was much, much more than their purchase price.

Oh, but I particularly loved my black star sapphire drop ear rings . . . except that my daughter Rowena has 'borrowed' them. And since then, she has 'borrowed' my black, onyx ring, too!

Poetic justice somewhere there. That'll teach me to be greedy.

ANOTHER SEMI-PRECIOUS JEWEL

This is not a story, just a memory . . .

Peter was a very successful business man; I met him and his wife over sixty years ago when I was an impecunious student. One day I remarked on Peggy's very pretty engagement ring, a wide gold band in the center of which was a lovely, large ruby. I, perhaps not very politely, commented on how expensive it must have been. She and Peter laughed, then told me the story behind it.

When they became engaged, Peter had no money but was determined that Peggy should have a symbol of his love. They went to Woolworth's and bought a sixpenny tin ring enclosing a large piece of red, cut glass.

For years, Peggy wore that ring until finally the tin broke.

Peter, of course, promised to buy her another, much more expensive ring, one with a real ruby. But that was not what Peggy wanted.

Their jeweler carefully separated that piece of cut glass and set it into the wide gold band she was now wearing.

Isn't there a phrase that says, "Price above rubies?"

GREG

An event happened while we were in Katmandu about which we didn't learn until later.

Greg had been staying with a friend across the road from our house. (The other three children had stayed with other families.) The two boys played in either home as the mood took them. Our servants were there, so we had arranged that this was fine.

The two were rather quiet and extremely polite when we returned from Katmandu. I was delighted and didn't think to question this remarkably docile behavior. When I eventually discovered what they had done. I wondered how they managed to bribe the servants to keep them from telling us what had happened.

Meanwhile, this saintly manner continued as days went by.

We had a long, screened-in porch where all the children loved to play, an area I rarely went in because it had become their own domain, and the servants kept it clean and tidy. This particular morning, while the children were at school, I entered intending to sit there with my morning coffee.

On the side nearest the car parking area, the wooden frame work looked different from usual. There was bright blue paint smeared on it. My oil paint!

I examined the wood more carefully. It was buckled and dented. I called the servants to question them. Somewhat shame-faced, they finally admitted the truth.

While we were away, Greg had wangled the car keys from the driver!

He and his friend had decided to go joy riding. There had been much crashing of gears while the other servant had come running out of the house protesting.

Thinking he was in first gear, Greg put his foot down on the accelerator. But the car was in reverse!

Crash. He drove backward, straight into the porch.

In horror at what they had done, those rather frightened boys decided to cover the damaged wood. What better than my paints?

When I heard what had happened, I couldn't help feeling relieved. If they had ridden out of the compound, they might well have had an even worse accident.

I mulled over what punishment I should give naughty Greg. For days, he must have been dreading the awful moment of discovery.

Ah! That dread was just what he deserved. I let him sweat a little longer! I don't think anything could have been worse for him. At last, one day he could stand it no longer and finally confessed.

I had a hard time not laughing. I know I should have read him the riot act, but after he had apologized to the driver and the other servants, and promised not to touch my oil paints again . . . or try to drive the car, I felt he had endured enough. Particularly that owning up at once would have saved him so much grief.

THE FLAG

In 1971, there were typical political growing pains of insurrection as East Pakistan sought for autonomy. We were living in Gulshan, a small, rather isolated area on the outskirts of Dhaka, the capital, and were reasonably safe from the scattered skirmishes: so we thought.

One evening, we got a phone call from our good golfing buddy, Delawah Shah, a general in the West Pakistan army.

"I'm afraid the troubles could be spreading in your direction. Make sure you keep the house locked up. Oh, by the way, if you have something black, hang it from your flag pole. Black is the symbolic color the rebels are using. No point in your risking their anger since this war has nothing to do with you."

Now this was rather disturbing news. We really had thought that we would be totally safe, for we had no part in the internal strife between the two parts of Pakistan. And, of course, one never believes potential danger will hit so close to home; surely Delawah was just suggesting unnecessary precautions.

But just to be on the safe side, I rummaged through drawers and cupboards to find something appropriate.

Now who has black items in their house? I had no black towels or tablecloths; no curtains or sheets of that color. In desperation, I finally opened my closet doors.

There, behind other clothes, I found just the thing. My seldom-worn cocktail dress. Truth to tell, it was a little too tight for me, which is why it had been relegated to the back.

I dragged it out and held it up for Gerald to consider. He laughed—no way was he going to let me know the worry he was feeling.

"This, I must see!"

He shook out the froth of lace and heavy satin, with the stiff lining under that created the full, bell-like shape. It really was a lovely dress.

We all hurried up to the flat roof of the house—the children and servants as well—to where the flag staff was. This was certainly to be an unusual, and to them, intriguing ceremony. With many giggles, I fastened the delicate shoe-string shoulder straps to the halyard and hauled my dress on high. It billowed quite elegantly in the evening breeze, like an overblown blossom: a fat, black tulip.

The laughter was good. No need for the children to have any qualms. We chuckled away as we returned to the living room: lots of witticisms about Mom's party pride, and total belief in the invincibleness of such haute couture. We went to bed that night, the house securely locked, and we slept.

Gerald did not go to work the next day. Neither did the children go to school. It seemed sensible since we could hear gunfire in the distance. Not that we were particularly disturbed, for we were far enough away, and untouchable . . . surely.

Mid morning, the gun fire was much nearer.

We all collected in one of the bedrooms and peered out of the window.

Between our house and the next was a field. Outside that house was a large crowd of people. Dancing, gesticulating people . . . firing guns.

Soon, flames appeared and we could hear screams.

Dear God! This was raw reality.

At last, cheering, seemingly satisfied with their murder and destruction, that angry mob moved in our direction.

We watched helplessly. Our gates were locked. So were the house doors. We had high walls around the compound, but would they be enough?

Still firing and shouting, the crowd stopped and began to beat on the entrance. By now, we had rushed in no little trepidation to another window to see.

Suddenly, one of the leaders pointed upward, to our flag pole. The tumult lessened. More and more of them looked up. We watched the obvious questioning going on among them.

The gun fire ceased and there was much shaking of heads. Finally, still gesticulating at that black flag, they turned away and straggled down the road.

You can imagine the relief we felt. It seemed we were to be left alone, for we were supporters of their cause . . . weren't we? My black dress, still fluttering on the flag pole, had done the trick.

Day after day, that poor, bedraggled cocktail pride hung in less and less glory as the rain washed out its starch. But limp though it became, it had served its purpose. No more were we disturbed by those angry people.

When three weeks later we were evacuated, I took it down and carefully packed it away. I had no intention of leaving behind that which had done far more for me than the mere wearing of it at some trivial cocktail party.

But as in so many of our experiences, the predominant memory is of laughter. The laughter of watching that black, black emblem flutter so incongruously in the delightful morning breezes.

THE MICE

A group of the expatriate wives determined to try to make enough money to have the children's' hospital painted. To this end, we decided to have a bazaar. Toys were always in short supply, so we created all sorts of amusing items. I made Dumpy Gonks. Large pillows with long arms and legs, and huge, laughing eyes on their faces. I hoped the children would get as much fun out of them as I did making them. They certainly sold well.

For the next bazaar, I created mice. It's amazing what you can contrive from scraps. I made large ears out of brightly colored fabric, and long tails from plaited wool. Soon I had forty ready for our next sale.

Then came war, and our city of Dhaka was in turmoil.

One night, we were warned to pack up ready to be evacuated. I and the children must leave. Once again, our good friend Delawah Shah!

I sorted madly through our possessions: things to take with us, items to be thrown away and others I hoped could be sent home later when the war was over. Our lovely rattan furniture, china, and washing machine (almost worth its weight in gold, so few of them were there in Dhaka) were to be given away after Gerald left.

Two days later, at six o'clock in the morning, my worried husband drove us to the airport.

Extraordinary situation, the sort that you don't really think is happening. Glorious, sunny day, the monsoon was over. Seventy-five degree temperature.

We drove to a rear entrance as the main gates were all locked. No one was on duty. No personnel to check our baggage or passports, not even a policeman was in sight.

We were to expect a British rescue plane to land to take us to safety: we and about three hundred British wives and children. It was not easy trying to keep cheerful since all our various husbands were to stay behind.

Guns were booming all over the place, so we parked as close to the runway as we could, that being as far away as possible from the bombs and bullets.

We sat on our suitcases and waited. Five hours we waited.

I had an enormous amount of luggage; all our golf clubs, stereo equipment, cases galore . . . and my forty mice. For some reason it had been important to me that I didn't leave them behind. All that effort and time spent . . .

Of course, one remembers the ridiculous in the middle of what I suppose could have been tragedy. Can you imagine crowds of yelling and screaming people waving madly up at the plane circling overhead? My kids thought it was fun. I have always believed laughter can get one through almost anything.

But I hadn't told them we were leaving Daddy behind. They just assumed it was another family adventure.

There was, of course, no indication from the airport tower that the pilot could land. He circled, watching the puffs of smoke from those wretched guns; and we tiny, dancing people, who were far too near the runway.

Finally, he zoomed down, flying low, hoping to avoid the fire.

The doors were opened and we were told to hurry. The engines were still running, for the captain dared not wait too long.

Startled and tearful good byes to Daddy, and all the other husbands and fathers; but no time to waste. Even my good old British-stiff-upper-lip was a little less firm. "Daddy will be on a later plane," I promised . . . I hoped.

It was just as well I didn't know that I would not hear from my husband for six long, long weeks.

Quite how and who had wangled for us to be on that plane, I never did find out, since it was really for the British contingency. Others on the Canadian project had left earlier for Penang in the Bay of Bengal, not waiting as we had, for Gerald had elected to stay behind to try to salvage something from the mess the country was in.

We bundled on board, I and my four children into first class. All the other wives and children clambered into the tourist section. Far too crowded, but the stewardesses were insistent, since those were what their tickets indicated.

Only four World Bank men joined us in our section, so we had dozens of seats to choose from, all to ourselves. My children soon settled down; they were quite used to Daddy's business schedule being erratic. And having so much space was as good as a playground.

I think at that point I collapsed. The stewardess served me champagne, which was so welcome! I don't remember, but I think I drank the whole bottle.

Most of our luggage had gone into the hold, but I had brought into the cabin a couple of cases for the journey. Coloring books, reading material, etc., which I dished out.

And the forty mice!

Once my children were settled, I began to worry about the crowded families in the tourist section. I asked if some of them could be brought into the front; all those seats to spare. No. That couldn't be allowed. Wrong tickets. Regulations, I was told. I peeped through the curtains and was appalled at what I saw. Little children were sitting on older children who were perched on their mother's knees. Now this was definitely against regulations, but the stewardess was adamant they must remain there.

Feeling so guilty at the comfort my children were enjoying, I wondered what I could do.

Ah. My mice!

Grinning cheerfully, I went through those curtains waving one and waggling its tail. "Who's being good?" I yelled over the crying. I wandered up and down the aisle, finally stopping at one pathetic child. Her smile was my reward.

A little while later, I returned with another mouse; and then another.

That journey took twenty-eight hours. An appalling, miserable journey. We landed at many different airports where we were forced to leave the plane to be examined. The whole emergency plan had been put together so hurriedly and was not on any regular schedule, so the pilot could not fly over various countries' air space, particularly as we had come from an area of war.

By the end of the journey, my mice had all gone.

But wives told me afterward that the excitement of wondering if the lady-with-the-mice would bring one to her child had kept many of those sad children happy through those long, weary hours.

Who dares to say that angels cannot come in all shapes and sizes? My little mouse angels never helped paint that children's hospital, but they brought a little happiness to other definitely deserving children.

GOLF AND GILES

But the almost two years between entering Dhaka and leaving were quite an experience, with many happy moments.

We played lots of golf and Greg, particularly, became extremely proficient. Most evenings, when Gerald had finished work, we would play nine holes. Each of us would have two Pakistani youngsters to help: a caddie to carry our bags, and the 'aggy-wallah' whose job was twofold: tracking the ball, and fetching it out of the lake. Golf balls were precious, and these little kids would dive into the water, invariably coming up with their trophy. Apart from their fee, they would receive a bonus if we still had the same ball at the end of the round, particularly as there was quite a considerable amount of water on that Dhaka golf course!

Now every golfer wants to achieve the ultimate, a hole in one.

One day, Giles, aged seven, did just that.

He was playing with me from the ladies' tee and we were on a par three, a hole surrounded by trees. He hit the ball hard, but not being straight, it ricocheted from one side to the other, then curled round the green, finally going into the hole.

"Wonderful, marvelous!" we cheered. "Only one stroke! A hole in one!"

But Giles looked quite disappointed.

"Does that mean I don't get to putt?" he asked.

. . . Which leads me to an earlier story about Giles

We try so hard to teach our children the realities of life, in as gentle a way as possible. At least, I did. Not always with the expected results.

The birth of my fourth child, Rowena, was by Caesarean section, so I asked the surgeon beforehand to make the stitches as neat and pretty as possible. I intended that my other three children should see the marvels of birth, and understand the brilliance of doctors, God and mothers, not necessarily in that order.

The dear, sweet man, amused by this modern mother, very carefully tied every stitch into nice, neat bows.

A few days later, when the swelling and redness had gone down, and my stomach had shrunk to more normal size, I proudly showed this little line of success to my other three children. Not

107

much in the way of comments, but they seemed to take it all in their stride. They did like the little black bows, though.

Of course, one never knows what brooding thoughts can remain in children's minds.

About six weeks later, we were coming out of church and getting into the car. Somehow, as the door was opened, Giles, aged four, caught the side of his face on the metal edge and cut a nasty gash.

A quick trip to hospital was going to be needed.

Well aware that tears might erupt at any minute, and wanting to distract him, I brightly told him he could have some of those pretty stitches that Mummy had.

I will never forget the look of absolute horror that appeared on his face.

"Does that mean I'm going to have a baby?" he asked.

ROWENA

. . . And since that last story was also about Rowena . . .

She was an extraordinary child. When she was born, the surgeon told that I would have trouble with her. I remembered how I groaned. What did he mean?

Apparently this was the first time in sixteen years of Caesarean surgery that he had brought forth a baby totally encased in the caul. This meant she had no loss of oxygen.

"She's going to be an extremely lively child," he told me.

How right he was. She never crawled. When she was barely nine months old, she just got up and walked. That in itself was rather cute, but as soon as she could get around, her inquisitiveness constantly got her into trouble. She climbed out of her cot with ease. I would hear this 'plonk' and then a sigh, followed by the patter of little feet. Door knobs were no trouble. With a big, beaming smile, she'd appear at the end of our bed.

In desperation, we added extra bars to her cot raising the barrier to her exit a good eight inches. We might have saved ourselves the money. Her climbing out just took her a little longer.

In the garden, Gerald built a corral; that was as good a name as any, for it had a fence over four feet high enclosing a four-foot-square play pen. I remember watching from the kitchen window that first day we put her in it. For almost an hour, that little madam piled up her toys repeatedly, patiently determined to get out.

And she did!

She was never a child who cried in frustration if she didn't achieve her goal, just persisted until she had accomplished what she wanted to do.

One day, she got out of bed early for her usual morning jaunt and, instead of coming into our bedroom as she generally did, she went into the kitchen and climbed on a stool to reach the freezer for ice cream.

I think I slept with one eye open; certainly one ear, and usually I heard her. This particular morning, I didn't.

When I woke and hurried into the kitchen, I found her sitting on the counter with the tub upside down on her head, ice cream trickling in all directions. We were having a particularly hot spring and I suppose she thought a little cooling was a good idea.

But that was just a messy moment with lots of laughs. Another of her escapades was not so funny. This was when I discovered that even locks were not sacrosanct to her.

She had come down stairs and decided that she wanted to go outside. Now this had never been a problem because we kept our doors locked—not to keep burglars out, but to keep Rowena in.

Pulling a chair to the door, she climbed up and turned the Yale lock.

This we didn't know she could do.

A thunderous knock on the wide-open door woke us.

An extremely indignant stranger was standing there with Rowena in his arms.

"Do you realize this child was walking up and down the road pulling her cart behind her? Some parents should not be allowed to have children. She might have been killed."

Leaving us stunned and silent, we watched him storm off to his car, which he had parked at the side of our garden.

In despair, we hugged our precocious bundle of mischief, and that day Gerald went out and bought more locks for the front door.

She even talked far too early. One day, when she was just a little over a year old, she went round the neighborhood inviting all and sundry to dinner. She had climbed out of her play pen, even though she had only small toys in there to play with so wouldn't be able to negotiate the fence, I had thought.

It's a wonder my hair didn't turn gray!

Lots of laughter from my neighbors when they called to check the invitation.

But she was not a naughty child, she just thought the world was there for her to discover. She's now an extremely busy lawyer working for peace and justice!

I suppose her enormous powers of concentration, and her determination to achieve her objective, are still standing her in good stead.

MY GRANDMOTHER'S RECIPE

It was the week before Christmas, I had planned an enormous carol party on the Sunday evening. I sent out invitations to all the children in our sports club inviting them, with parents, to our house. Some of the families I had asked to represent one of the 'Twelve Days of Christmas', partridge, geese, gold rings, etc., so we could all sing to their antics. Every one seemed quite excited by the prospect of this huge family get together with Beef-on-Weck, cookies, cider and hot chocolate to follow.

On Saturday, we set up two oil drum halves in the front garden and filled them with firewood. We prepared the food, and shifted much of our furniture up stairs as I knew we all would end up in the house, for the winter weather could be bitterly cold. Our Lowery organ was maneuvered close to a window, which could be opened ready for our church organist to send forth wonderful Christmas music.

Later that evening, when all was ready, leaving strict instructions to the children not to eat any of those yummy sandwiches, Gerald and I quickly dressed for our Company Ball. I remember how tired we both were with all the carol preparations we had made, but this Ball was rather like a command performance, no excuses allowed.

In fact, we thoroughly enjoyed the dancing, but were quite exhausted when we dragged ourselves home in the early hours.

We slept like logs.

At eight-thirty the next morning, Gerald suddenly woke, sat up, groaned, and looked at me in horror.

"Oh, my God. I've just remembered. I asked them all to brunch!"

"Who? When?"

"The president, the other vice presidents, and all their wives!" He gulped. "All ten of them . . . at eleven o'clock this morning!"

You can imagine my consternation. "But I've no extra food in the house. The fridge is full of the children's food for the carol party . . ." As you can imagine, I could have killed my husband. But that would have to wait!

"Go to the store, quickly; shrimps, salads, cheeses, ice," I made a list.

My two boys rushed upstairs and began to bring down the furniture, my daughters scrambled around with dusters and put out dishes and cutlery, and I, helplessly, opened the fridge door . . .

I had two hours to work a miracle! But what with?

Ah, there at the back was a two-pound packet of sausage meat intended for breakfast. Maybe I could make a savory something or other. I needed a hot dish. But what could I add? I slammed open cupboard doors and searched. I found raisins, cranberries and a jar of sweet relish.

What else I mixed in that sausage meat, who knows?

I added stuffing to bind it all together and give it a little extra flavor, and I think I added a little brandy - and a few prayers. Anyway, I stirred the lot together, crammed it all into a bund pan and shoved it in the oven.

I whipped up some rolls; they'd fill a gap if all else failed.

I lit the fire in the family room where Greg set out the drinks trolley, I put some of the cider I'd prepared for the carol party on the stove to simmer and made a jug of Bloody Mary's; at least I had enough tomato juice for that.

Christmas cake and cookies of which I had plenty, added festive color to the table, and Gerald's shopping expedition had produced salads, and lots of shrimp, which I spread over ice in a huge punch bowl.

Finally I took the sausage 'thing' out of the oven and up-ended it onto the waiting plate.

Oh dear!

A grey splodge! And our guests were due to arrive any minute.

Back to the cupboards again. Ah, a jar of salsa! Nice cheerful color. I poured it over the top, The 'thing' definitely looked better. Then I opened a tin of apricots (almost the same color as the salsa) and placed them around the plate, adding a dollop of mint jelly to each one. I put a tiny silver mug in the opening at the top and stuck in a candle and some sprays of holly.

Now what could look more Christmassy? We stood back and laughed! Julia Child, eat your heart out!

. . . But the proof of the pudding is in the eating . . .

Our guests arrived, shivering from the cold winter weather, and were soon warming themselves with the hot cider and the Bloody Mary's, and toasting their toes around the blazing fire. The Christmas tree was twinkling brightly and carols were merrily pealing forth; all was cheerful good will.

But our guests were hungry; it was time to eat.

Rachel was delegated to serve the 'thing'; - not too much in case it was ghastly. I watched as forks dipped in. I held my breath. Oh dear, the moment of truth.

"Mmm, this is so good, so tasty, What is it?"

Good Lord! Our guests came back for more. Even the men. Soon it was all gone!

"You must give me the recipe, this is delicious . . ." I could hardly believe it, all the women were clamoring for a list of ingredients..

Now this was one secret I had no intention of sharing. How could I? They would probably gag!

"How kind of you, but I'm sorry, this is a recipe of my grandmother's, and she has forbidden me to share it."

"Oh, what a shame, What does she call it?"

"Er . . . (Quick thinking), her Christmas Savory Surprise!"

I hope the snorts of laughter from my family were hidden in the contented chatter of our guests as they praised me. To think my culinary reputation was made on splodge!

The party seemed to be a success, but I begun to wonder if they would ever leave, It was almost four o'clock when they finally finished their thanks and wended their slightly tipsy way to their cars.

Now began another marathon. Gerald rushed out to those waiting half-drums, large bottle of lighter fluid in hand. Sensibly, we had stuffed fire lighters among the wood, and the tarpaulin we had covered them with had kept them dry. Loud whoosh, luckily no singed eyebrows, and stage one was underway.

The two boys yet again shifted the surplus furniture upstairs and Rachel and Rowena rushed to clear the dining table making it ready for the next meal. I heated the Beef-on-Weck, ready to put them out on platters later. I added more cookies to the table, and refilled the cider pan. I filled the urn with chocolate for the children and set it ready to simmer.

Mad change of clothes, loud speaker switched on sending forth Christmas music so everyone would know we were ready to party. The carol sheets were set out and the organist arrived.

Phew!

But what a wonderful evening that was. I think every child we had invited came, many with two parents. Our 'Twelve Days of Christmas' performers had excelled themselves. Each had created cardboard signs, birds' heads, or costumes, the fathers holding up

113

their participating children all the better for the audience to chime in at the right time.

"More, More. Again. Again." The carolers loved it. We must have repeated it at least four times.

As the evening grew colder and the fires died down, we all went into the house and sang until our throats were dry. Cider and hot chocolate, delicious Beef-on-Weck and Christmas cookies, sighs of happiness.

I remember the last carol we sang as our guests were leaving was 'Oh, Holy Night.' To hear the voices drifting on that cold, crisp winter evening as the carolers wended their way home made me forget my promise to kill my husband when that day was over.

Yes. All was right in the world. I really did (finally) feel 'Peace and Goodwill to All Men' . . . even to my husband!

ANOTHER PARTY

A couple of stories about Rachel . . .

Of course, much as we love our children, we are not blind to the fact that they don't always grow up to be perfect; but even so, I have usually found that they bring more laughter than anger. Not that I necessarily let them know that, for chastisement must be delivered when warranted.

Rachel wanted a graduation party.

I agreed but laid down a few rules. She must clean up any mess, and not break anything, the usual behavior all parents expect. And no alcoholic drinks in the house.

She and Giles (nineteen months her junior), promised they would be little angels. This I doubted, but they were fairly trustworthy children. Gerald and I went to sleep in another part of the house where we wouldn't hear any noise.

When we came down in the morning, everything was in apple pie order. Dishes had been washed, the place vacuumed. Indeed, you wouldn't have know there had been a party.

Pleased, I complimented them, hoped they had a good time, that their guests had enjoyed themselves. Since there were no telltale cans or bottles in the garbage, I praised them for keeping to their promise of no alcoholic beverages in the house. Smug glances from one to the other.

"Just as you said," they answered.

I should have guessed.

Later that day, I went onto the deck. There was a steep slope beyond, and usually I would not even bother to look over the edge.

This time, I did.

I didn't count them but there must have been dozens and dozens of beer-bottle caps lying there.

I know I should have been cross; after all, prevarication really is the same as lying. But as they said when they eventually, puffing and blowing, climbed back having collected all those pieces of metal, they had obeyed the letter of my law. As they had promised, nobody had drunk the beer in the house, though they had blessed their luck that it had been a fine, warm evening.

THE ENVELOPE

When Rachel went off to college, I had given her the same instructions I eventually gave to all my children. All fees and their meal tickets, we would pay for, but no pocket money. Each child was expected to have a thousand dollars, which they had earned, in the bank for that purpose. I had even informed them that if this goal were not reached, then they just would have to forgo a further education until they did.

So off Rachel went, determined to be careful, because I was adamant that it was no good coming to me for extra money. Cruel Mom that I was, but lessons of life need to be learned early.

Christmas Day. All the family were home and it was time to unwrap the parcels under the tree.

Amongst the ornaments and tinsel strewn over the branches was a white envelope addressed to Mom and Dad.

It was from Rachel. Curiously, Gerald and I opened it

It contained $46.75.

Of course, we thanked her, but she could see we didn't understand the significance.

"That was left over from my meal ticket." Casual reply.

"But, Darling. You could have kept it. I didn't want you to return it."

"Of course I had to. It was yours."

Sweet honesty. Moments like this are treasured by Moms the world over. Worth much more than $46.75.

GOOD HOUSEKEEPING

Gerald was going on a three-months tour of duty in Ethiopia. I and the children were to stay at home. We weren't too happy about this, but it was summer vacation time, and I promised we would do all sorts of fun things to make up for Daddy being gone.

Before he left, my husband sat me down and went through all the bills I would have to pay while he was gone: electricity, telephone, mortgage, etc. He filled my account with house keeping, and money for incidental expenses. There was a slush fund I could dive into if necessary, and in the last resort, I could use our savings account. I became well aware that my sweet husband was less than sanguine about my capability of managing, for he always took care of family finances. Truth to tell, I was a bit miffed. I wasn't a spend thrift and rarely went over my housekeeping allowance.

And so he left. A few tears but lots of brave smiles.

Determined to make the best of the situation, we began our summer vacation.

The children and I did have fun. Not expensive fun. We had plenty of parks and playgrounds nearby. The occasional pizza, which normally I didn't allow them to have, and ice cream, were treats they enjoyed.

The months passed. I watched every penny. I was going to show my husband just how well we could manage without him looking over my shoulder. The children's pocket money was adhered to strictly. I bought no new clothes for any of us. I paid every single bill promptly. Oh yes. I was doing well.

But as it neared the time for Gerald to return, I was growing worried. Somehow my money was not lasting as well as I had hope. Yet I had wasted nothing on frivolities, and had rarely splurged on a McDonald's outing. I tightened my proverbial belt and warned the children that the last couple of weeks were going to be 'slim pickins'. Of course I could have dipped into the slush fund, but there was a principle here. I was not going to have any "I told you so" remarks.

The day Gerald arrived, I was down to pennies. Once our greetings were over, I admitted to him that I needed my next month's housekeeping check immediately. I told him I hadn't touched any other money. I proudly showed him the list of bills I had paid.

He looked down at them and began to chuckle. "No wonder you're broke." he said. "You've paid an extra month's mortgage."

I didn't tell the kids. I think they would have shot me.

117

CONSEQUENCES

I suppose I was a tough Mum in many ways, but my children were too precious to me, particularly as we traveled so much.

One of the first rules I had was essential, for in crowded streets and strange countries, we needed to establish what to do in certain circumstances. If they somehow lost sight of us, they were to look around for the highest point—a wall, perhaps, and climb on it and wait. They were not to search for us, for if they tried to, they could become even more lost. We would come back to the point we had last seen them and all would be well. No need for them to have any concern at all.

Of course, rules are much more fun if they are a game, and my rambunctious children were not averse to playing tricks on us if the opportunity arose.

One day we were visiting a zoo, and Greg, by then about seven, was lagging behind, showing his little sister various animals, while I was pointing out others to Giles who was still a baby.

I turned around . . . and those wretched two were no where in sight.

But they had been there only a moment ago. I backtracked, they would be round the previous bend, perhaps. Certainly they couldn't have gone far.

No sign of them.

Now when one lays down rules, one should remember them, and what those rules require. Yes?

I didn't. I kept going back and forth, Giles' pram becoming harder to push. Zoos are noisy places, and though I called and called, there was no reply. Other mothers with their children were looking at me, some with sympathy, others with disapproval. How careless a mother I must be.

I suppose no more than a few minutes passed, but it's easy to become frantic when you're scared.

I stopped, leaned against the high fence that divided the walkways. Totally bewildered, I didn't know what to do.

Then I heard a chuckle. It came from above my head. I looked up, what I should have done in the first place. There were two mischievous faces grinning down at me. Those rascals had climbed onto the park seat at the other side of the fence.

"You told us to climb high if we were lost." All innocence. Of course they hadn't been lost. "It was just a game, Mummy." To them, it had been such fun. Little devils!

I had another rule; or rather, a non-rule. I called it consequences.

One of them might ask if they could stay out late on a school night. I would give full permission, adding a 'but'.

They would groan. "O.K. What are the consequences?"

That was the easy part, "You won't have studied for your test . . . you'll be too tired for that sports game . . . what if you don't wake up in time and miss your bus?" Nothing more needed to be said, and that child stayed at home.

I secretly was rather proud of my lesson teaching.

Of course. It didn't always work.

Rachel, by now sixteen, wanted to get her driver's license.

I went through the usual rigmarole. "Of course," (Now here came my list of consequences) "The roads are much too dangerous; I don't trust the other dummies on the road; beside that, you have to go through Drivers' Ed school because I won't teach you, for you are too young; I don't approve of teenage drivers . . ."

This time, I wasn't convincing her, though, so finally I put my foot down and said no. Not at all my usual tack.

"I will not support you in this," I said. I was adamant. "I will not help you in any way because I love you too much to risk you getting into a car and having an accident."

Silence.

No more begging or pleading.

I really thought I had won!

Some weeks later, I discovered what this little madam had done when she brought to my, with great pride, a signed statement that Rachel Ann Nugent had passed her exam with flying colors. She was now eligible to get her license.

Not only did she have her certificate, so did Giles, her fifteen-year-old brother. Now he was neither old enough, nor had he asked my permission.

Just how had these little monkeys finagled this?

These two children attended a school that did not have driving instruction, so one day they got off their school bus at the local high school, found the instructor there, spun a sob story about this cruel mother and persuaded him to give them lessons . . . for free.

Not only did he give them the full six-week course, when the classes were over, he dropped them off each day at the end of our road.

When Gerald heard about this, he thought it was hilarious. Of course, he backed them up wholeheartedly.

"Certainly Rachel shall get her license!"

The only thing I could do to save face was to refuse to take my daughter to her test, but Daddy did the honors. Rachel always could twist her father round her little finger!

These two children thoroughly enjoyed putting one over on their Victorian mother; but it is interesting to note that they both are extremely careful drivers. They might have beaten me, but they were never foolish enough to risk bringing their mother's retribution on their heads.

I may have lost the battle, but I won the war.

THE CAKE

Our children secretly planned a fiftieth anniversary party for us while we were visiting them in Connecticut. They told us nothing about it, wanting it to be a complete surprise.

And it was; particularly the cake, which was bigger and more opulent than the one we had when we got married. Rowena had won in a raffle a certificate for a wedding cake. She decided how appropriate it would be to change the order to an anniversary one for our party.

This gorgeous concoction, made from scratch with the best ingredients, was tiered and decorated and far too much to eat on that occasion, so we packed away two tiers, froze them and brought them back to Tennessee.

Not long after, old friends from England whose spouses had died, decided to come over to the States to marry each other.

We were thrilled for them.

Pat, whom I had known for almost seventy years, was especially dear to both Gerald and me, and Peter, her husband-to-be was a love. Of course, we wanted to make their wedding day special. We planned a party to which our local friends happily promised to come. Of course, there had to be a cake.

Ah. Our anniversary cake.

Somehow, it seemed such a special touch to use it, much more so than a store-bought cake because of our long years of connection; it would be a mixture of nostalgic thought and long memories; a tying together our years of association.

A dear friend, one of the guests, another Barbara, who is a dab hand at decorating cakes, promised to come over the evening before the wedding and titivate any part of it that needed touching up.

Oh dear! We all gasped when we lifted the lids from the cakes that had been standing out to defrost. The exquisite icing furls of roses and leaves had become misshapen, squelchy splotches. My heart sank.

There was only one thing to do, open a bottle of champagne.

But I should have known nothing phased dear Barbara. She had brought a prepared batch of butter icing just in case. Carefully scraping much of the old icing away, she placed one tier on top of the other and began to work.

More champagne!

I watched in fear and trepidation, I had thought my nostalgic idea had been so good. Dumb woman! Yet we had no choice but to carry on. No wedding can be complete without a cake.

When the side and top had been smothered with the butter icing, Barbara got out her fancy nozzles and began to embellish with intricate decorations while we watched. Talk about Phoenix rising from the ashes!

We were well into our second bottle of champagne by now.

By one o'clock in the morning, we were singing a mixture of 'For she's a jolly good fellow,' and 'Happy days are here again.' That cake was superb, better than it had been. Wonderful, wonderful Barbara. She even added flowers around the base to make it more original.

Of course, at the wedding everyone praised the cake, which was quite delicious, and nobody seemed to mind that it was made over from another occasion. Indeed, all the loving thought that had gone into its presentation made it much more special.

But there is a story going round . . . "Did you hear the one about the second-hand wedding cake . . . ?"

THE NIGHTDRESS

This is a story over which I have chuckled many times, but never shared with Gerald until our fiftieth wedding anniversary. I had feared he might be angry with me.

Years before, when we had lived in Buffalo, my husband used to have lunch where models paraded showing the latest fashion available for purchase. Regularly, he would buy something and have it sent home for me. Equally regularly, I would return the gift because it was the wrong size, color or style. Lots of grateful thanks and appreciation, of course.

One day, I was telling a friend about these gifts and she gave me a good telling off.

"You mustn't keep sending them back. He must be very hurt, Not every husband is as kind and thoughtful as yours."

Feeling rather ashamed of myself, I promised that the next gift he sent, I would keep.

Sure enough, a little while later, another parcel arrived.

I opened it and took out the most gorgeous negligee; a froth of delicious lemon chiffon—yards and yards of it. A lovely yellow rose was stitched at the extremely low cleavage, and a wisp of lace formed a tiny bolero-like jacket. The whole garment was definitely honeymoon wear.

I tried it on, even with my extra pounds, sexy was the word! After four children, I hadn't really expected my husband to have such romantic thoughts.

Of course, this was a gift I had absolutely no intentions of sending back.

When Gerald came home that evening, I greeted him with exuberant delight. "It's absolutely gorgeous!" I enthused.

"Good," he said, "I knew you wanted a new dress for the Ball this weekend."

"But . . . " Stunned, I opened my mouth—and closed it, "The Ball?"

What on earth could I say.

"Th . . . thank you, honey. How thoughtful of you."

My mind was racing; how could I explain without hurting his feelings? How do you tell your husband he has made the blunder of the year?

Of course, you don't!

I just knew that somehow I had to wear it to the Ball: but did I really dare to do so? Surely everyone would know just what it was: a seductive, filmy, soft negligee.

I called various friends who were going to the same Ball. What should I do?

Go for it! They thought the whole idea was terrific.

"Lift the flower a little," said one.

"Wear a petticoat under," said another.

"I've got some long earrings that'll match." said a third.

I was becoming a little more convinced.

"The rest of us will look so dowdy and conservative wearing the same old black thing."

"And the men will drool!"

That did it.

So to the Ball I went: yellow negligee and all!

Of course, I got some strange looks, but by the time my dear friends had praised Gerald's choice and told him how lucky I was to have such a loving husband, he was preening his good taste.

Dear man.

Would you have deflated him by chuckling at his mistake if you had been his wife?

Of course not.

But there is one rather sad ending to my story. I could never wear that negligee (sorry, evening dress) to bed.

Thirty years later, when it was my turn to reply to the toasts at our fiftieth wedding anniversary party, a little imp of mischief persuaded me that now was the time to confess.

I'm not sure who laughed louder, my children, my friends, or my dear, loving husband.

FOOD, GLORIOUS FOOD

I've no idea what Oliver Twist would have thought of some of the food I've eaten over the years. As far as I know, I've not eaten rats, cats or dogs, but during the war we ate horse meat and whale steaks. My mother never told us until after those meals were over: wise woman.

Frogs legs! In Africa, torch light at night had been responsible for catching many a delicious meal. I once asked Kwaku how he prepared . . . er . . . dismembered the eatable parts. He said, "Madam no want to know." I accepted his word, but I noticed he had a large meat cleaver in his hand as he reached into his sack to remove one of the squirming frogs. Delectable as they are, they've not been my favorite food since then.

We've eaten python steaks, not as tender as those narrow filets of pork my husband likes so much, or his favorite cod, but very similar. And talking of fish, the Bay of Bengal has fresh water almost a hundred miles from the shore, so all sorts of varieties were available, beautiful flavors, which our Pakistani cook prepared deliciously. But there was one meal where his laborious efforts were quite startling.

We had people to dinner this particular evening, and after the first course was finished, the bearer asked if Hussein could carry in the next one because he was so proud of what he had created. It was, according to him, a very special paté. Always willing to give praise when it was due, naturally I said yes.

In he strutted, so proud of himself. He placed the platter in front of me.

On it was a large fish, plenty for all of us.

How I managed to keep a straight face I don't know.

Dragging out somewhat extravagant compliments, I told him he had really excelled himself, and so pleased was I that I would serve. I would be the bearer. (There was no way I could allow him to take that plate closer to our guests.)

The two servants beamed as they bowed their way out of the room, happy that Madam was so delighted.

Delighted? Actually, I was horrified.

Then we all began to laugh . . . smothering our giggles as best we could.

I looked at the fish head, still in its raw state, its malevolent eye looking at me, and at its tail, equally raw, propped up with tooth picks. Quite enough to make us shudder.

But those were not causing the laughter. My creative cook had removed the body, cooked it and moulded it back into its original shape, then decorated it with gills.

Carefully, mathematically placed gills.

Dozens and dozens of them.

These gills were sliced, slivered and identically shaped potato chips, carefully and crisply fried. Each one had been equally carefully placed overlapping the next.

That wouldn't have been too bad, perhaps, but each one had been dyed . . . in alternate colors . . . bright red and green!

Now what was I to do? None of us could even bear to take a taste. But we couldn't offend Hussein who must have worked for hours on his masterpiece.

Yet somehow we had to pretend we had enjoyed it!

Then my ever ingenious husband hit on the solution.

We spooned a tiny amount onto each plate, pushed it around with our forks, then removed the remainder to the bathroom where it was disposed of down the toilet. We crumbled pieces of the tiny toast quarters, which were to be eaten with our fish, onto our plates so that it appeared we had wasted none of our paté . . . I was so glad that our guests were very good friends. And equally glad that dear Hussein could boast to his own friends of the remarkable success of his original paté! In my mind, I can still see that monstrosity, and to this day I don't particularly like dyed food, or fish pate!

One of the meals I always enjoyed was a 'West African Country Chop' (chop meaning food). It was the staple of most Sunday lunch parties.

This was basically curry and rice. It might be chicken, lamb or beef and could be mild or hot according to one's taste. But what I mostly enjoyed, and was intrigued by, was the way it was served.

The meal was usually set up as a buffet. At one end of the table was the rice, the curry being at the other end. In between would be as many as thirty small dishes, each containing fruits, nuts or vegetables. Some would be fried—bananas, tomatoes and onions; others, roasted such as shredded coconut or salted peanut. There would be a least a dozen dishes of fresh fruit cut into small pieces: in all, a wonderful combination ranging from sweet to sour.

Now came the fun part. The guests spread rice on their plates first, smoothing it out until the whole surface was covered. Then they would take small spoonfuls from each colorful dish, making sure they did not overlap. When the rice was hidden, the curry was spooned over, again making sure it left none of those little pieces visible.

Next one found a comfortable chair and began to eat.

Of course, as one dived into the food, one had no idea just which flavor would mingle with the curry. Would it be sharp lemon, sweet pineapple, crunch onion, or even hot, hot peppers? Part of the entertainment was listening to the surprised—and one hoped—delighted oohs and aahs. Nothing humdrum or boring about that meal!

After the curry, 'jungle juice' was served. This was a bowl of every type of fruit grown in our gardens. So soothing—necessary after the heat of that delicious main course—and probably the 90 degree temperature.

And so to bed . . .

I was always amused that it was quite expected for everyone to depart as soon as the dessert was finished. Time for an exhausted sleep. Ah, those were the days . . . It was just as well that that form of West African Curry was served mainly on Sundays.

MORE GOLF

Marvelous character builder. Just as you think you've got the game licked, the golf gods knock you down . . .

The ladies golf team at our club in Orchard Park was to play another. I groaned when I discovered my opponent was Lancy Smith, once the US amateur champion: way out of my league.

Ah well, it was a lovely day and Lancy was such a sweet lady she would never laugh at my poor efforts, but I groaned as I watched her drive go screaming down the fairway, she easily made a birdie.

Then, wonders of wonders, so did I!

The next hole was a par three. Of course, Lancy birdied that one, too.

Extraordinary. I, also! I could hardly believe it. Two birdies in a row was practically unheard of for me.

Now came our monster par five.

The green was on a plateau with deep bunkers on either side. I played my second shot—a 'Hail Mary' if ever there was one—and was stunned to see it land on the edge of the green. Again a first for me. Good heavens! I had the opportunity to make an eagle, or at least, another birdie.

Lancy's shot landed in the deepest bunker!

Of course, by now I was feeling decidedly smug; I was playing the best game of my life. I stood complacently watching Lancy attempt to get out of the sand, knowing I was going to win this hole. Already I was thinking, "One up."

But oh dear, those golf gods must have been doubling over with laughter. Lancy stroked her ball nonchalantly onto the green and it dribbled right into the hole. She was the one who got the eagle.

And I . . . I three putted.

Talk about deflation. I double bogeyed the next hole, and my game went from bad to worse. I didn't win, or even tie, any more holes. My visions of greatness disappeared into the mist.

Ah well, I did at least have a dream . . . for a moment.

Another time, those gods must have laughed even harder.

Gerald and I were playing a course where there was an abundance of water. We prepared to play a particular hole where the tee was immediately backing onto one of the lakes. In front of us was this nice, straight, green fairway, a par three. Gerald teed off.

128

Shouts of glee. He made a hole in one. Now every golfer longs for such an achievement; this was my husband's first. You can imagine how proud and pleased for him I was. Now it was my turn.

Still gurgling my delight, I teed up and waggled my club ready to strike the ball.

I wasn't really paying much attention to my shot, was just re-visualizing that hole in one, allowing my club to waggle backward and forward . . . backward and forward . . . Then I unwittingly made contact. I hit that ball . . . backward. And where did it go? Straight into the lake behind us!

So my husband's proud story of a hole in one became even better. Do you know of any other couple who both had a 'hole in one' on the same hole on the same day?

But I do have one more story where the gods were particularly kind.

It was my sixty-fifth birthday and I was feeling somewhat low, for surely any golfing ability I had would be fading; now I was officially a senior citizen.

Gerald and I went out to play, as we did most days, with a couple of friends.

I expect I was relaxed, for what was the point of trying? Dreams of greatness were things of the past.

We reached the fifth hole, an evilly long par five where the fairway has masses of bunkers and drops over five hundred feet. Usually I consider myself lucky if I scrape a bogey.

I managed two reasonable shots and was still on the fairway.

Next, I hit my third shot vaguely in the direction of the green, not even bothering to look where it landed.

Yells from the others. That ball had dropped right into the hole.

An eagle! "Happy birthday," was Gerald's laughing comment.

We went to the next hole, a par three over a deep chasm with a devilishly sloping green.

Quite stunned, I watched my ball fly right up to the hole. I could hardly believe my luck as I sunk the put.

The next hole, a par four, I did the same. Another birdie . . . and on the next, also.

An eagle and three birdies in a row. Wow. Five under par through four holes!

Of course, my euphoria didn't last; I expect the golf gods woke up. No more birdies, but I did end up with one of the best rounds I had ever played.

But my purpose in telling this story is not to boast about my prowess . . .

Later, I was listening to comments on the television by Arnold Palmer who was bemoaning the fact that he was nearing sixty-five and his good golfing days would be over. I longed to tell him,

"Not true, Arnie. Never give up. The best may yet be to come."

THE AFRICAN CHURCH

Being a Baptist, in our early married life I rarely went to the Catholic church with Gerald. Only when we moved to Accra was I able to attend a church of other faiths including my own.

This, basically, was 'Church of England' and was attached to the school where I taught.

But there was a decidedly unusual aspect to this building. Because the various missions in Accra had no other house of worship they could use, each Sunday one or other of them would take the service.

Quite a lesson in ecumenism.

We actually had seven denominations. Church of England, of course, Baptist, Presbyterian, Methodist, Congregational, Plymouth Brethren and Salvation Army. Gerald was highly amused by this and would tease me about 'sounding brass and cymbals', for cymbals were certainly sounded when the Salvation Army members joined our choir.

But eventually, when we returned to England, I attended the Catholic Church because all our children became Catholics. I never had a problem with this because of the ecumenical lesson of that dear little African building. I had learned that the true essence of each religion was much more important than the different practices. I coined a phrase, which I have used many times when asked why I do not become a Catholic.

"We are all going up the same mountain, we merely go up different sides."

When we came to Tennessee, I became much more involved in the local Catholic Church than I had intended to be. We needed a much larger building and, because of my architectural background, I was roped in. Three years of fund raising and planning eventually led to the construction of our present church.

Many had been the nights that I had worked well into the wee hours of the morning on my drawing board, so it was with considerable relief when the new building was completed.

Now like many of my stories, there's a twist. One day, knowing ours was a mixed marriage, one of the church members came up to Gerald and asked him a deeply serious question . . .

"Why don't you become a Catholic like your wife?"

Hmmm. I'm not sure that my husband thought this was funny. I know I did!

MY EMBARRASSMENT

This supporting of the Catholic Church has always been something I have done, and this same support I have given to my children, encouraging them in their faith.

But sometimes, there have been rather amusing consequences.

Rowena was to be confirmed, and she gave me instructions regarding the sash she had to wear. This was bright red on which I was to stitch white felt indications of religious significance, and her name. I carefully cut out the word PEACE, and a white dove; then the letters ROWENA.

As I sat at the back of the church with the other mothers, I couldn't help noticing how many Teresa's and Mary's, and John's and Paul's were the names on the children's sashes.

"I hadn't realized how many of our kids have Biblical names." I commented.

"But those are some of the names each child is supposed to choose; they don't have much choice."

"Each child chooses?" I was bewildered.

"Yes. The saint who will protect them through life."

Oh dear. I wanted the earth to open and swallow me up. I hadn't know, hadn't understood, had just thought . . .

As Rowena walked down the aisle to the rather ancient bishop who was blessing each child, I wondered what he would say.

At last. it was my daughter's turn.

The assisting priest, with a puzzled expression on his face, bent close to the old man and whispered in his ear. Much consultation and shaking of heads.

Finally, with a rather expressive shrug, the bishop raised his hand and blessed Rowena.

I wondered if I had blighted my child for life, but dear Gerald searched through his book of saints and found that there was a French saint with a name that sounded almost like 'Rowena.' Near enough, we thought. I was much relieved!

We swallowed our guilty chuckles . . . and my embarrassed shame.

TYPHOONS, HURRICANES AND TORNADOES

In 1970, a terrible typhoon tore north through the Bay of Bengal and smashed its way all across the southern area of East Pakistan. The loss of life was simply appalling. Well over a million people were drowned by the huge tidal wave, which swept over the flat land; some say the number was far greater.

We huddled in what we hoped was our solid and safe house as the howling wind buffeted the doors and windows. We lost power, of course, and the blackness of the night frightened even Gerald and me. We heard the sounds of flying debris as it crashed against the walls, and dreaded what we would find when the morning came.

The area was a dreadful mess, of course, but Mother Nature can be quite amusing, even in her fury. We had a high wall around our compound. All along it were tall trees. As if she were using a carving knife, the old lady had meticulously neatly sliced each tree parallel with the top of the wall. Those stumps looked almost indecent, as if some decadent power had striped them naked.

But perhaps that was my warped sense of humor, or was it the almost hysterical relief that we were safe?

When, years later, we were living in North Carolina, a tornado ripped through our area. It landed on three houses, ours being the middle one. We were away at the time. We rushed back, fearing the worst. The other two houses had enormous structural damage and ours was totally hidden by trees that had been uprooted and piled against the walls. But when they were removed, we were unutterably relieved to discover that we had almost no damage. Those branches had actually protected us.

Much later, one of my college students had her trailer torn from its foundation by a tornado. It was picked up, then dropped completely over their car in which she and her family were sitting, having just come back from town. She said it was the most extraordinary feeling, as if that trailer were protecting them from further damage. So easily could it have been their car that the tornado attacked. Then who knows what might have happened to them?

Years later, I had another experiences of the power of Mother nature. I was driving down the main street in Crossville when a tornado ripped along the road, tearing up everything in its way . . . and almost got me. A vast stream of water and masses of sand and shale buffeted and battered my car, and a huge Shell sign flew twisting and

133

turning, just missing my window. The car was a write-off, but I was safe.

At another time, yet another tornado whooshed up our mountain. It flung itself at our house . . . Again we were blessed; not too much damage.

With the law of averages, surely this cat's nine lives must be running out. But perhaps there has to be some moral here about only the good die young . . .

Or is it this sense of invincibility that my childhood upbringing bred in me, which usually protected me from the trauma of fear?

Yet we all remember stories like these. In so many of them is the incongruous.

And the incongruous, I love!

During the Second World War, a bomb blast blew in the side of a house, and the owner, a dear old lady, still in her bed, was wafted into the air to land in the grave yard next door. When the local wardens reached her, she was singing hymns. I wonder if one of them was 'Nearer my God, to Thee'?

I sometimes think—and hope—that I have had my share of being a little too near!

VACATIONS, GLORIOUS VACATIONS

During our time in East Pakistan, we went for a week to Hong Kong. The length of Gerald's tour had been extended and we needed to stock up on clothing of which there was very little available in Dhaka, so we took empty suitcases.

Of course, we filled them. Actually we went a little crazy. Talk about leading a thirsty man to water . . . We bought golf shoes (hand made overnight) clubs, camera and projector, watches, a pearl necklace, toys (Giles bought the biggest set of hot wheels he could find), and goodness knows what else. When we returned to Dhaka, we loaded all our bags and parcels onto the table in the customs shed and I, with bills of sale in hand, waited for the duty officer to tell me the worst.

"You are returning from Hong Kong,Yes?"

Here it comes, I thought. Everyone knows how tourists shop in Hong Kong.

"Yes, I'm afraid we've bought rather a lot."

"This is all second hand, yes?"

"Er, no. We've just bought it all in Hong Kong."

"Surely they are second hand?" The duty officer repeated his question.

"Er, well, I . . ." What should I say?

"Have a good day." He grinned at me as he marked every bag and parcel with a white chalk mark.

In no little bewilderment, I turned to Gerald who was standing with the children. He looked equally surprised. He had been waiting, credit card in hand, ready to pay the enormous amount of customs duty he expected.

But it seemed there was none!

The officer waved to a porter to collect our bags and parcels and moved on to the next waiting tourist. We had finished all that was required of us, apparently.

Now whether the man couldn't be bothered to cope with such a mountain of luggage, or whether he liked the look of our faces, I never knew. But the thought passed through my mind that perhaps we should have bought more from that wonderful Aladdin's cave called Hong Kong

But there was another side to our visit that touched us all, particularly Gerald.

We went to the golf course on Victoria Island. Lovely, peaceful surroundings on the shores of Repulse Bay.

Here we learned the bitter story of what had happened there thirty years ago. The Japanese had come; this beautiful place had been a prisoner-of-war camp. Gerald had fought the Japanese in the Burma Campaign and he had seen many atrocities. His uncle, a doctor, had died in such a camp. He was burned alive.

My shopping spree didn't have quite the same flavor after that.

But in recent years we have had other lovely holidays. Giles and his wife Yvette rented eleventh century Todi Castle in Italy. Giles' party included their two sons, we two sets of grandparents, Rowena and her husband Bryan, and Rachel whose dear husband Chuck had agreed to stay home looking after their daughters still in school.

What an extraordinary place. Our bedroom must have been the Duke's, for the enormous, ancient bed had a carved ducal crown over the headboard. There was a huge armoire equally as old. It was a bit shivery to sleep in the actual bed where over five hundred years of royalty had slept! The windows were narrow slits set in feet-thick walls, but thank goodness the bathrooms were good, modern American style.

To reach Rachel's bedroom, one had to traverse a decidedly rickety outer walkway to the top of a tall tower. She loved it. What tickled me most was when she leaned out of the narrow window, just wide enough for those ancient archers to shoot their arrows. She draped her long blonde locks over that rough, gray stone. "Rapunzel, Rapunzel, Let down your hair," we called to her with much laughter.

The following year, Giles and Yvette rented a chateau in France. This was equally fascinating, probably fifteenth century. Gerald and I had a bedroom, dressing room and bathroom bigger than most of our house. The others had equal accommodation. Such luxury was something neither Gerald nor I had ever known. It reminded us of one of the stately homes of England.

But the room that tickled my sense of humor was the kitchen. It was huge. I paced it out. Sixty feet long. We actually had to shout to each other if we were at opposite ends.

Oh! But the lovely, crusty French bread we ate in that echoing place, with cheese that made our mouths water, and plenty of French wine, of course.

136

And all around us, vineyards, and apricot trees, cows in their pastures, sweet smelling hay, and cheerfully chirping magpies and swallows. Perhaps at eighty we are too old to return, but we both wistfully remember those halcyon days.

Dear Giles and Yvette, you were so generous to include us.

The other children have been equally generous, though perhaps holidays with them have been less exotic, but just as full of love. We have been blessed.

We stayed with Greg one Christmas when the weather was so appalling that we hardly ventured out of the house; terrible blizzard conditions. I spent the time reading all of Greg's Dick Francis novels. Thank you, Greg, for introducing me to them. Now I avidly watch for each new one as it comes out. That is certainly a holiday I will never forget.

Was this the Christmas when we decided to have ham instead of turkey? I seem to remember putting it in the oven and forgetting it. When we came back from an outing, it was burnt to a crisp. No! Surely that never happened? That is certainly a holiday I will never forget.

One Christmas we spent with Rachel and Chuck. On Christmas morning, we all went to church and to visit a friend leaving Chuck at home watching the turkey. Somehow we were not clear about the instructions we gave him. Thirty minute basting time had been mentioned. When we returned, we found a very bored Chuck sitting by the oven, kitchen timer in front of him. Every thirty minutes over a period of four hours he had religiously basted that turkey, then reset the timer for the next thirty minutes. We never did tell him that we had only meant that turkey to basted thirty minutes before the end. As you can well imagine, it was the most gloriously browned turkey, and the most tender.

It's now a point of honor whenever we sit down to a turkey dinner to say, "Lovely turkey, but not as good as Chuck's."

Rachel once threw a party, which we were unable to attend, but to me it was very special. She invited a book club friends and chose my first novel, Winter's Eden, as the book to read and discuss. Dear, sweet daughter.

We've spent many Christmases with Bryan and Rowena and often both our families have been there. Food is always in great abundance as everyone chips in with salads, turkey, ham, and a plethora of delicious cookies and desserts. Rowena's signature dish is whole tenderloins wrapped in leeks, one of her only two specialities.

I'm always impressed with its success since Rowena has never aspired to kitchen duty. Impressing the judge in court, yes, but cooking is definitely not her thing.

We have to admit we are glad that Bryan, who owns a restaurant, does most of the everyday cooking when we are visiting. It's a joke on those occasions . . .

"Is Rowena cooking dinner tonight?"

"Not unless it's pork chops" one of us will say, "they're the only thing she can cook!"

Secretly, I think she has kept up that myth. 'Why keep a dog and bark yourself?' Or more to the point, 'Why have a marvelous chef for a husband and not sweet-talk him?'

But Rowena is the greatest party-thrower!

Recently, she and Bryan decided to celebrate their twentieth anniversary. She sent out one hundred and fifty invitations. Would you believe, all but one of those invitees came? That shows how popular her parties are. Definitely, 'the hostess with the mostest'.

There was one especially poignant moment. They renewed their marriage vows.

. . . And what better garment to wear than a brand new, exquisite wedding dress.

My daughter never does anything by halves.

OUR GRANDCHILDREN

How could I forget that glorious moment when I held my first grandchild in my arms? Victoria was just twenty-four hours old. Feelings of awe and overwhelming love. Such a good baby, too. As she grew, she caused us much laughter with her feisty, eager enjoyment of life and the people around her.

When she was just two, I was showing her a picture of a bird on the National Geographic cover. I had never been given much to baby talk, but this time, I slipped up.

"Oh, look. What a lovely ducky!"

Quickly came back, with her nose in the air . . .

"That's not a ducky, it's a lune." She was right!

(I expect Rachel had told her, but Victoria really loved her moment of superiority.)

One college professor at Duke University will always remember her, and so will the other students there that day. We were all at the garden party celebrating Giles's graduation year. A few of us were standing chatting to this rather important dignitary who had an Einstein-like hair style; white and as bushy as steel wool.

Suddenly, across the grass came three-year-old Victoria. She rushed up to the professor, eyes sparkling.

"I know who you are, you're the Wizard of Oz, and I've seen you three times."

I wonder if he has forgotten that startling moment? We certainly never will.

Next came Amanda.

One Christmas we were all seated at the dining table waiting for Chuck to serve the turkey. Amanda was all of nineteen months old.

Grampa loves the leg, so the first one was passed to him. At least, it started in his direction.

Eyes gleaming, Amanda stuck out her two little hands and grabbed it. Now you have to realize this had been a particularly big turkey, and this was an equally big leg. Indeed the fat part was about the size of Amanda's head. Her little mouth stretched open as wide as it could and she tried to bite it. It wavered and wobbled, bumping into her little face, dripping the delicious juices all over her.

Total serious concentration! No matter that we were laughing our heads off.

Finally, she sighed. "Too much," she said as she dropped it on her plate. "You eat it, Grampa."

Five years later, at Giles's wedding, he rented a London tourist bus to take the guests to the reception. The two girls had been so good all through the ceremony, but now the fun started.

All in our finery, we climbed to the upper deck. It was a beautiful day, sun shining, birds singing, and two happy bridesmaids called down to people on the side walk,

"We're going to a party."

Of course, why stop with that? All the way through the park, down Fifth Avenue, they sang and chatted to all and sundry. And the New York crowds responded. I think Amanda, particularly, thought the whole journey was just for her benefit. Oh, she loved the people, and, of course, the people loved her. Certainly that day Amanda didn't know a stranger, and she never has since.

Three years later, Giles and Yvette had their first child. One day when Eamonn was five, he came home from school rather depressed. Concerned, Yvette asked him what was the matter. It seemed that one of the boys had teased him.

"I don't like boys," he said. "Please can I have twin sisters?"

Yvette prevaricated as mothers do. Then came Eamonn's next question.

"Doesn't Daddy have a couple of sperm left?" Yvette couldn't wait for Giles to come home so she could tell him the latest funny.

My, oh my! Does sex education really start this early.

Obviously, Eamonn has a very curious mind. When he was seven, he became fascinated by planets, astronauts and space stations. One holiday, he sat me down beside him and demanded that I looked up information so that he could write on his computer an article on Mars. He smothered me with a huge pile of books. I did my best. It would have helped if I knew anything about the wretched planet in the first place!

Staccato questions.

"How far is it from Earth? What's its size compared to Venus? Is there ice? What kinds of minerals?" And those were the easy ones!

As I thumbed my way through those books I was sure I would suffer from carpel tunnel syndrome. Those tomes were heavy!

Recently, Eamonn heard that the NASA program may be shutting down. One sad little boy.

Trying to cheer him up, his Daddy promised to buy him a large poster for his bedroom. Surely it would be another picture related to space travel.

No. He is changing his interest now; he wants a poster of the periodic table. When I next go to visit, I just hope he doesn't expect much chemical knowledge from me. He'll be out of luck!

Ian didn't say much when he was very small; having an older brother probably didn't give him too many opportunities. But when he did speak, I was always so impressed.

Ian loved long words and absorbed them from who knows where. One day when he was three, as he was carrying his usual load of toy cars, he dropped one.

"Please pick it up," said his tidy-minded mother.

"I'm not an octopus, you know." he replied.

Recently, when Yvette was explaining to him how some people work at night, he summed up her description. "Oh, they must be nocturnal people." Not bad for a five-year-old!

At Halloween, he made a rather sad comment explaining that he had not enjoyed himself. "I don't like going up to people's houses that I don't know, and asking for things that don't belong to me."

Sensitive wisdom there somewhere.

He asked his mother recently, "Why do we have four witches in the pledge of allegiance?" Yvette wracked her brains. "You know, 'One nation, under God, four witches stands,'" said Ian.

Never a dull moment! We are so lucky to have such lovely grandchildren.

CROSSVILLE

Just as I was asked when we attended that cocktail party in Montreal why we had come to Canada, we have often been asked what brought us to Crossville.

It was actually a sign showing azaleas.

We were living in Atlanta where we had retired to what had been a quiet, peaceful community, but the area had developed so much that we decided to look for a place in the more rural countryside. One such exploratory weekend, we drove to Tennessee.

Seeing this most attractive sign as we drove along the I 40, which pointed an arrow up a mountain, we decided to see just what else was up there.

It was all of four miles to the top of that winding road, and we were entranced by what we saw. The wide panorama was magnificent. As a child, I had loved the views across our Yorkshire moors and had always longed for a place where we could see far into the distance.

Half an hour later, we drove back down the mountain having bought a parcel of land. We have never regretted that spur-of-the-moment decision. We love our aerie in the sky and have been here for twenty-two very happy years.

But first, we had to settle our affairs in Atlanta. Finally, we began to build our house on the edge of the escarpment and hoped to settle into lazy, peaceful retirement away from the noise of big cities.

Ha! How the gods down through the years have laughed at our intentions.

Gerald discovered the local community college that was just opening.

"My wife's a teacher," he told the administrator.

And that was that.

I had had no intention of going back into the classroom, but how could I refuse? And neither could Gerald when he, too, became aware of the need.

Now opened a new world.

I began to teach English development courses to those who were not ready to enter their first year of college, and my husband agreed to teach math. His vast experience as an engineer was invaluable. Years before, he had been asked to help out at the local high school when the chemistry teacher had become ill. Since the students were studying the atom, Gerald explained how an atomic power sta-

142

tion worked. The students were fascinated, and my husband was hooked.

Many happy days he had spent there teaching from his practical knowledge whenever a math or science teacher was absent.

Thus, my husband decided that he, too, having enjoyed that experience, would teach at Roane State. During his years there, he was able to bring to life the rather dull subject of algebra by explaining its practical use in the everyday world outside the classroom.

Our students, whose ages ranged from eighteen to sixty, were the most rewarding we have ever taught. Their eagerness and determination were a joy.

In many instances, this determination hid an almost desperate desire to do well. Most of them were the first ones in their family to go to college, and many of them had achieved little more than an elementary standard of education. Their lack of confidence in their ability was sad; encouraging them to have faith in themselves was the most important lesson we could give.

And seeing them encourage each other added a new dimension to our teaching. I remember how the members of one class dived into their pockets to help a student who was in desperate need. She had eight children, one, partially blind. Her husband had left her. Food stamps as well as cash were shared, and these same students approached their various churches for donations, which paid her electricity bill.

Of course, others helped, but I've never forgotten the generosity of those students who had so little themselves.

Or their kindness.

I had a student who had been an alcohol and drug abuser and was trying to turn his life around. There would be ugly scenes, explosions when he lost control, tears of remorse afterward. Yet I never once saw disgust or irritation on the faces of the other students. They encouraged and supported him. Years later I met him again. Big beaming smile as he told me of his present life. He had graduated from college and was now a respiratory therapist with his own clients . . . and I have to admit I had thought he would never succeed.

But we had much laughter in our classes, too.

I was discussing procrastination and set the students an appropriate piece of homework. Each one was to select an activity they had been putting off and complete it, then tell in the next class what they had learned from the experience. Of course, there were promises to tidy their bedrooms . . . clean out the garage or weed the garden, but one student asked rather tentatively if he could do something different. He worked long hours, and with school work as well, he hadn't taken his wife out in ages. Could he do that?

All the students thought this was a terrific idea and we, in some amusement, looked forward to hearing about his 'date' and what he had learned.

Next time we met, there were some of us who wiped away a few surreptitious tears as he told his story.

When he told his wife about his 'home work', she, of course, was delighted; but it was the reaction of his children that had amazed him. They had pooled together their pocket money, made an appointment at the hairdresser's for their mother, done extra chores so she could spend time getting herself ready, and promised to do all their homework and be little angels while their parents were out. He told us how the children insisted he dress in a suit with collar and tie in keeping with the pretty dress his wife was to wear.

"And where did you take her?" we all clamored.

"We went out to dinner and then to the cinema."

Big sheepish grin.

"We sat on the back row and canoodled."

Such a lovely, sentimental, appreciative sigh from his audience. And what better lesson to explain how we should not procrastinate.

But that's not the end of the story. Years later, I was teaching a similar class about this same problem of procrastination and told of this particular student's 'date'.

A small voice piped up from the back of the class.

"Mrs. Nugent, that's my Dad."

I hesitated, longing to ask questions.

She continued.

"They've never forgotten. Dad says it's the best homework he ever did."

"And does he still procrastinate?" Of course, I finally had to ask. After all, that was the purpose of the class.

"I don't know about that," was her reply, "but he takes Mom out regularly now."

Aha! It seems my lesson had its merits.

Seeing our students blossom was our greatest reward.

Recently we met a lady who had been in one of Gerald's first classes. She was just finishing up her thesis for her doctorate. It had taken over twelve long years to reach her goal, and she told us if it had not been for my husband's dedication and insistence that she was far more capable than she had believed, she would never have reached it.

I have often wondered just what guided us to Tennessee, that our intended retirement years were not yet to be.

In my own classes, I began to spend more and more time on creative writing, using the students' own life stories for the double purpose of building their confidence and recognizing they actually could write. They gave me some extraordinary results, and these students, as they shared their experiences in life, began to have stronger feelings of pride.

The local library decided their senior citizens also had stories to tell, so I gave a six week course, which extended long beyond my original intended time. The members of the class became so proud of their efforts that we compiled a book of their stories to share with their families. Many of those senior citizens are still meeting ten years later, and some are having considerable success in writing novels.

One rather poignant story that happened only a few weeks ago . . .

I had gone to one of these meetings, One of the ladies who had struggled over her writing had finally finished a story for her grandchildren. To our delighted pleasure, when she read it to us we all were so impressed. This was a much better piece of work than she had previously done. Of course, we praised her, happy at what she had achieved.

That afternoon she went home so excited at her success. She ate supper, went to bed . . . and that night she died in her sleep.

Of course, we were all rather shattered, but when I talked to her son a few days later, he told me, "She died one happy lady. She had so much wanted to get that story finished, and she did."

What better epitaph could there be?

During this time, I started a new career. My dear, sweet husband had long been encouraging me to spend more time writing, and he took over most of the house work. He's turned out to be a marvelous cook, and he even takes care of the laundry.

At first, my scribbles were just an amusing exercise, but realization that the years were passing, I finally, regretfully, gave up my much loved teaching and began to concentrate seriously on my own writing. Thus, I began to write novels and have written four; but

I have not forgotten those stories the students wrote, or the pleasure they found in sharing their memories.

So since they say, 'Put your money where your mouth is,' at the urging of my family and those students, I began to gather these various stories of my own life.

Remembering the sometimes funny experiences, and even the less happy ones, has brought a new rejuvenation of mind, soul and spirit.

After all, though the rest of my time on earth may be short,

*You don't have to be dead if you're **only** eighty.*

It has always been my aim to encourage others to write short stories.
Please forgive me if I am being presumptuous
by including the following.
(This has been the basis of my classes.)

Helpful Hints for the Aspiring Writer

Short stories in general seem to have become an endangered species. Most fiction writers feel they must jump right into the deep end with an earth-shaking novel. That's fine if you know how to swim, but the greatest of novelists learn the rudiments of their craft through the tight discipline of the short story; indeed, some of the finest literature in the English language can be found in the short story form. Its brevity makes it seem deceptively easy, but it presents a challenge that can be formidable.

The novel allows the writer to develop, to expand and to explore his settings and characters at leisure; but the short story needs rapid establishment of scene, situation and people. It requires merciless pruning, an economy of words, the strictest of limitations, yet it must create action, a vivid scenario, an absorbing atmosphere, an empathy of feelings, all with the minimum of words. To tell a story solidly and entertainingly, to grasp immediately and hold the audiences attention, to create a visualization, all in a few pages, is far from easy; but it is the best way to sharpen the writer's skill.

Consider these suggestions to help you become a better writer.

Are you achieving your goal, succinctly and clearly? Is your story easy to read and understand with just enough background to enable the reader to picture the events? A good exercise before you start to write is to close your eyes, picture what you want to write about, then 'chat' on paper, letting your ideas tumble forth with no attempt to organize or worry about grammar.

When you are stuck, close your eyes again. You will be surprised at the unexpected phraseology you use. This natural writing will have a flow to it that careful construction does not have. Remember, you are writing the story. It is your story. You tell it the way it sounds in your head. This exercise is also useful as a check when you think you have finished your story. Have someone read a section, then tell you what they 'see'.

147

Your purpose in writing this story must always be kept in mind. Decide before you start on the final intent; whimsical humor, pathos, a harsh tragedy, whatever. If your story is to be humorous, write with a smile on your face. You will soon recognize if your sentences are too heavy.

Be ruthless in cutting unnecessary verbiage. Just as too much sugar or too much salt can spoil a meal, so do your readers not want to eat through masses of detail to get to the essence. On the other hand, they need that picture to appreciate the joy (or misery) of the action, so concentrate on the highlights of your story. Your reader needs to laugh, cry or shudder at your description. When you start, do not be afraid of the thousands of memories that will converge and muddle clarity and chronology. 'Chat' as fast as your fingers can write. Only by putting your thoughts on paper can you begin your masterpiece.

Language. As you progress through your pruning process, use direct and simple language. Preciseness comes only with simplicity. Avoid pretentious, academic jargon. Write the way you speak. If you wouldn't use a word or phrase in your every-day speech, then don't use it in your story. Be extremely careful and sparing in the use of descriptive words. Make sure each word means exactly what you want it to mean. Similes and metaphors are often much more vivid than a plethora of descriptive adjectives or adverbs.

You have a mind; you have a memory; events have made life-long impressions on you. What more do you need to be a writer?

Sincerity: Dig deep and write what you know. Don't contrive. Never undervalue your writing. Through our stories, we pass on ideas and traditions from one generation to another. Every story you write has some sort of message, a message important to you; so therefore, it is important to the world. Be proud of your efforts, but use simple language: one of Shakespeare's most compelling speeches begins, 'To be or not to be, that is the question.' Notice the number of letters in each word.

Sentence value: Never include a sentence that does not expand on the character or advance the action. Pretty words for no purpose have no value.

Music: If your own words are musical and lyrical; for example, native American, Irish, or even colloquially curious as phrases used here in the hills of Tennessee, use their metaphorical color. And though a hard-headed northerner may have a language as harsh as a hammer, even he can drive home a point in his own way. Never feel that standard English is the only acceptable style. All va-

148

rieties of speech are beautiful. Your writing will sound most real when you write like the person you are, but write accurately.

Teaching: We feel we are on dangerous ground if we try to teach our readers; that is presumptuous, but our audience wants us to simplify, clarify and explain enough so that they can understand. To bake well, it's no good just piling the ingredients into the oven; we have to know how to mix and blend as much as necessary, with as light a touch as possible, to make that cake not only eatable but delicious.

Finally, no one really cares how well or badly you express yourself as long as you have enchanting things to say. It is easy to tidy up and dramatically punctuate a story, but all of your heart has to be in every word.

Other Works by Barbara Nugent

Winter's Eden
A late winter's storm forces Amanda Arundel's car off the road causing her to seek shelter in what she believes to be a hotel. There, a secret, international, political meeting is taking place. The angry owner accuses her of illegal infiltration and holds her prisoner, refusing to believe she is just a nurse on vacation. Only after an incredible adventure in the mountains of Afghanistan does she discover the purpose of that meeting and just who is her captor.

Gulls Walk
Devastated at the sudden death of her grandfather, Rowena Pentraegon determines to hold on to her inheritance, Gulls Walk, an Elizabethan Manor house. Having almost no money, she decides to rent one of the wings to an autocratic Spaniard who seems to have only contempt for her, What is the reason for his dislike? Why are others so determined to own her home? If only Gulls Walk's ancient mystery of buried treasure were true, would that solve her financial problems?

A Business Proposal
Rachel Cameron's whole world crumbles when her fiancé breaks their engagement. The owner of the mining company where Paul had worked is furious at him for abandoning her. His sense of responsibility determines that he will help her rebuild her shattered life; hence, his unusual business proposal. But will she agree?

Macedonian Icon
Researcher Jane Percy Brown is fascinated by the extraordinarily vivid pictures of antiquities and artifacts taken by photographer Caulder Macgregor. Needing more material for his book, he asks her to come with him on his travels. But is there a deeper reason behind his search for the unusual? Is the sinister stranger who follows them the dangerous instigator of kidnapping and attempted murder? During exploration of strange, ancient places, three brave men, a Croatian, an Albanian, and a Macedonian, determine to protect Percy and Caulder and prevent a terrible destruction that could spread fear across the world.

Made in the USA
Lexington, KY
20 March 2012